Revitalizing General Education in a Time of Scarcity

A Navigational Chart for Administrators and Faculty

Sandra L. Kanter
University of Massachusetts Boston

Zelda F. Gamson
University of Massachusetts Boston

Howard B. London
Bridgewater State College

with
Gordon B. Arnold
Montserrat College of Art

Janet T. Civian
Wellesley College

Foreword by Frederick Rudolph

Allyn and Bacon
Boston   London   Toronto   Sydney   Tokyo   Singapore

Executive Editor: Stephen D. Dragin
Editorial Assistant: Christine Svitila

Library of Congress Cataloging-in-Publication Data

Revitalizing general education in a time of scarcity : a navigational
    chart for administrators and faculty / Sandra L. Kanter . . . [et
    al.].
       p.   cm.
    Includes bibliographical references and index.
    ISBN 0-205-26257-0
    1. General education—United States—Case studies.   2. Education,
    Higher—Aims and objectives—United States—Case studies.
I. Kanter, Sandra L.
LC985.R48   1997
378.1´99´0973—dc20   96-9703
                                                                   CIP

Printed in the United States of America
10   9   8   7   6   5   4   3   2   1   00   99   98   97   96

For David Riesman, from whom we have learned to look closely

Contents

▶

List of Figures, Tables, and Boxes

Boxes

▶

Foreword

When the long entrenched classical course of study began to erode—or to be enhanced, depending on one's view of the matter—the Yale faculty in 1828 issued a report that could be considered a first statement of what a general education ought to be (*Reports,* 1828). The Yale faculty were driven to the curricular drawing board by challenges to the dominance of Latin, Greek, and mathematics and by efforts to make room in the course of study for modern languages, laboratory sciences, modern history, and literature.

More than a century later, Harvard's "Red Book" (The Harvard Committee, 1945) was a gesture hurled in the same direction as Yale's 1828 report. By then, however, general education had become a movement with adherents, detractors, a great many variations, and an uneven record of successes and failures (Rudolph, 1977). Harvard's trumpet call of 1945 went unheeded, but the unstructured and fragmented incoherence of the college curriculum that both Harvard and the general education movement sought to repair continued to trouble the academy.

With its core proposals of 1978, Harvard returned to the curricular wars and specifically to the general education battlefield (Rudolph, 1993). In the 1980s the National Commission on Excellence in Education (1983), the National Endowment for the Humanities (1984), and the Association of American Colleges (1985) issued reports that helped to shape the environment in which the colleges and universities that are the subject of this book entered into their experience with general education.

In the early decades of the 19th century, before the curricular stirrings that triggered the Yale report of 1828—and long before the advent of academic majors and discrete vocational programs—all college education was general *and* professional. Young men went to college knowing that they would all have more or less the same curricular experience on their way to top positions of leadership in the professions—church, law, medicine. The same general learning was shared by all; specific professional skills might be learned on the job, as an apprentice, or at the few schools devoted to theology, law, or medicine. Most clergy, lawyers, and doctors entered the professions without a B.A. degree; the leaders in the professions, on the other hand, not only held the degree but also shared the general learning certified by that degree.

The colleges and universities whose curricular experiences are revealed in this book are in one sense victims of the history that shattered the comfortable certainties of two centuries ago. In another sense they are partners in a widely shared effort to put the general, the common, the shared learning experience of an earlier time back into a college education or at least to keep some element of it there.

General education is a slippery concept. The authors of this book make no effort to define closely what general education is or what it ought to be. That task, an unenviable one, has been undertaken by the colleges and universities that have used general education in recent decades as an instrument for treating their ailing courses of study. The evidence here is that while there may be no one way to define general education, there are indeed many ways. Here it is allowed to encompass long-established and uncontroversial distribution requirements as well as intricate core programs and complex interdisciplinary courses capable of wrenching professors out of accustomed practices and certainties.

The context in which general education enters into the curricular life of these colleges is one of limited resources, overextended faculties, and academically less talented students. These are nonelite and unselective institutions nervous about their hold on their constituencies. They are also the kinds of institutions where the great mass of American young men and women pursues a bachelor's degree.

If general education often seems to elude the grasp of curricular reforms at these institutions, or if at best it seems only partly to fulfill their hopes and expectations, the very effort to define it has provided focus and community to otherwise incoherent, fractured institutions. There may never have been an academic *community* anywhere in the United States, except perhaps at the early Johns Hopkins. However, outsiders looking at the academy in any of its varieties have always sensed the differences that significantly separated insiders from those outside the gate. Whether those differences meant that inside the gate there was a community is another matter. Inside the academy, community has been challenged, even subverted, by a whole range of noncurricular forces—religious enthusiasms, departmental rivalries, the celebration of diversity and multiculturalism, the tension between intellectual and anti-intellectual values, between academic and athletic priorities. General education, this study suggests, is not a sure cure for these ailments, but if it is applied wisely, the patient doesn't die, may improve, and on the whole feels better.

The authors have used their interviews and visits to campuses to establish, in five chapters, carefully drawn generalizations on how marginal, struggling colleges and universities have used general education as a path to renewed vitality and vigor. In addition, 15 close-ups of individual institutions provide portraits of their general education experience as they try, against great odds, to fulfill their obligations to themselves, their students, and their communities.

Skeptics of educational research might fault this study as only confirming what common sense has long told the rest of us. They would be wrong. The portraits of individual institutions in the throes of curricular reform reveal nuances, surprises, differences, and paradoxes beyond the reach of common sense. If there are indeed elements of the obvious in social science fact and theory, so much the better. It is important that would-be reformers be alerted to the obvious, for that is often the overlooked element that thwarts their designs.

One feature of general education not likely to occur to common sense is its usefulness as a way of differentiating one struggling college from its struggling competitors. There is evidence in this study that just such an effort to establish a distinguishing identity led many a college to undergo the pains, uncertainties, and tensions that went along with new curricular structures. However it is understood, general education gives an institution attempting to define itself an opportunity to differentiate itself from its competitors. If wealthy state universities choose to be defined by heavily subsidized athletic programs and players, why shouldn't struggling colleges and universities do it with less expensive and more honorable adventures with the curriculum, even if those adventures invite uncertainty and tension?

While tension between vocational faculties and liberal arts faculties was common to the process of embracing or enhancing general education, there appears to have been little or no attention paid to ways in which vocational instruction can be informed by liberal concerns and ways in which traditional disciplines can be made vocationally pertinent. At colleges where a vocational focus had long been central to their community role and to the recruitment of students, general education ignited instant conflict.

"Is general education reform worth the effort?" the authors ask. The question is more than rhetorical, although the mere publication of their book may be the most definitive answer. This study may be read in many ways for many reasons.

Certainly it is a cautionary tale. It is also a contribution to the sociology of academic decision making. It is a guide to modes of survival on the edge. It is a study of free-enterprise higher education in a free-enterprise society, accented by competition, winners and losers, and the absence of supportive overriding national social values and purposes. Here are institutions straining to be the best they know how, often thwarted, persevering, and not always succeeding. It's a book about good guys who don't give up and who are better for having tried.

Frederick Rudolph
Professor of History Emeritus, Williams College

▶

Acknowledgments

The authors are grateful to the Exxon Education Foundation, which funded the General Education Implementation Project, of which this book is a part. The project is a multiyear study of how colleges and universities with limited resources have implemented changes in their general education programs. We deeply appreciate the continuing support of the foundation's former program officer, Richard Johnson, now of the Alliance for Higher Education in Dallas, Texas. Caryn Korshin has been an able successor to Mr. Johnson.

Support for the project and the book was secured by the New England Resource Center for Higher Education (NERCHE), whose director, Zelda F. Gamson, was crucial to its conceptualization, creation, and completion. NERCHE provided the resources, clerical assistance, physical space, and intellectual comradeship that made this book possible.

For inviting the authors to present their findings at conferences and to write preliminary papers, we thank the American Association for Higher Education; the Association of American Colleges and Universities; the Association for General and Liberal Studies; the Association for the Study of Higher Education; and the National Center on Postsecondary Teaching, Learning and Assessment.

We are grateful to the faculty, staff, and administrators

of the 15 campuses we visited, who graciously welcomed us to their campuses and gave freely of their time for interviews. We have not mentioned them by name because we assured respondents that confidentiality would be respected. Without their cooperation, however, we would have been unable to do this research. We would like to thank also the contact person on each campus who helped set up the interviews, provided background information about their institution, and attended to many other details. Some of these people have since gone on to other positions and other institutions. For help in arranging visits to their campuses, we thank Frank Bisher, Albertus Magnus College; Henry Fanning, Bridgewater State College; Antoinette Iadarola, Colby-Sawyer College; Alan Marwine, Green Mountain College; Paul Abajian, Johnson State College; Alice Whiting, Johnson State College; Daniel O'Day, Kean College of New Jersey; Jolene Schillinger, New England College; Theo Kalikow, Plymouth State College; Loretta Shelton, Roger Williams College; David Leigh, Seattle University; Stephen Spector, University of Bridgeport; Michael Mills, University of Hartford; Jack Armstrong, University of Maine at Machias; Howard Cohen, University of Massachusetts Boston; Elizabeth S. Blake, University of Minnesota, Morris; and Mary Ruth Brown, University of Minnesota, Morris.

Colleagues at the University of Massachusetts Boston have challenged our thinking throughout the research and writing for this book. We are grateful especially to Howard Cohen, currently provost at the University of Wisconsin— Green Bay; Richard Freeland, now president of Northeastern University; Russ Hart, professor emeritus of English; Sheila Post-Lauria, associate professor of English and associate provost; Woodruff Smith, dean, Faculty of Liberal Arts, College of Arts and Sciences; and Patricia Davidson, dean, Undergraduate Education, College of Arts and Sciences.

Members of the Think Tank on Liberal Learning convened by NERCHE from colleges and universities throughout New England helped us test and temper our ideas. Institutions and colleagues who brought us in as consultants taught us much about the vicissitudes of general education reform. These include Bellamine College; California State University; Lake Superior State College; Temple University, most especially Nancy Hoffman and Bill Nathan; the University of Massachusetts Lowell, especially Peter Blewett; and the University of Rhode Island.

We also want to recognize the many important contributions made by members of the research team who left the research project before the writing stage. Linda Eisenmann, the founding director of the project, who is now at the University of Massachusetts Boston, contributed significantly to the conceptual framework of the research design. Jana Nidiffer, now at the University of Massachusetts Amherst, helped to design the survey and carried out early visits to campuses. Daphne Layton, of the University of Massachusetts President's Office, and Robert Ross, of the Harvard University School of Public Health, also worked on the project in its early stages.

We acknowledge the continuing and generous support of NERCHE staff: Mary-Beth McGee, now at Boston University; Deborah Hirsch, associate director; Sharon Singleton, executive assistant; and Catherine Burack, director of the Faculty Service Project.

To Barbara Baird Ryan, our editor extraordinary, our abounding admiration.

We thank our families for their forbearance and encouragement.

▶

Biographical Notes

Gordon B. Arnold is associate dean of academic affairs and associate professor of social science at Montserrat College of Art in Beverly, Massachusetts and research associate at the New England Resource Center for Higher Education, University of Massachusetts Boston. His experience includes general education curriculum planning and the design and teaching of interdisciplinary liberal studies courses. His current research focuses on faculty labor relations in public colleges and universities in New England. He holds a B.A. degree from Clark University and a Ph.D. in higher education from Boston College.

Janet T. Civian is director for policy research in the Office of Institutional Research at Wellesley College, Wellesley, Massachusetts and director of the Pathways Project for Women in the Sciences at the Center for Research on Women, also at Wellesley. She is a senior associate of the New England Resource Center for Higher Education, University of Massachusetts Boston. She has worked at Harvard University with the Assessment Seminars and as research associate for the Derek Bok Center for Teaching and Learning. She holds a B.A. from Wellesley College, an A.M. from Stanford University, and an Ed.D. from the Harvard Graduate School of Education.

Zelda F. Gamson is professor of education and the founding director of the New England Resource Center for Higher Education at the Graduate College of Education, University of Massachusetts Boston. She is the author of numerous works on social policy, organizational innovation, and educational reform, including *Liberating Education* (1984); *Black Students on White Campuses: The Impact of Increased Black Enrollments* (1978), with Marvin W. Peterson and Robert T. Blackburn; and *Academic Values and Mass Education* (1970), with David Riesman and Joseph Gusfield. Gamson attended Antioch College and the University of Michigan, where she received an honors degree in philosophy and an M.A. in sociology. She holds a Ph.D. in sociology from Harvard University.

Sandra L. Kanter is an associate professor and faculty member of the Doctoral Program in Higher Education at the University of Massachusetts Boston. The author of a number of articles on general education, she has consulted widely with colleges and universities on their general education curricula. Kanter has held positions in academic administration at the University of Massachusetts Boston and at Lesley College. A senior associate of the New England Resource Center for Higher Education, University of Massachusetts Boston, she founded its Think Tank on Liberal Learning. She received a B.A. degree from Connecticut College, a master's degree in city planning from the University of Pennsylvania, and a Ph.D. in urban studies from the Massachusetts Institute of Technology. She was a Loeb Fellow at Harvard University.

Howard B. London is professor of sociology at Bridgewater State College and senior associate of the New England Resource Center for Higher Education, University of Massachusetts Boston. The author of several books and articles on higher education, London has served as a consultant to several colleges and universities and is a research consultant to the National Center for Urban Partnerships. He is also the project director of a study, sponsored by the Ford Foundation and the Spencer Foundation, of eight urban community colleges from which students transfer in unusually high numbers to four-year colleges and universities. London attended Bowdoin College, from which he received an honors degree in sociology. He holds an M.A. and a Ph.D. in sociology from Boston College.

▶

Introduction

BACKGROUND AND PURPOSE

During the 1980s, 75 percent of all U.S. colleges and universities changed their general education requirements, instituting more rigorous standards for graduation and tightening the curriculum (American Council on Education, 1988). By the mid-1990s, even more institutions had done the same, as they experienced the double bind of increasing constraints on their resources and ever mounting pressures from their publics to be relevant and (simultaneously) to maintain the quality of higher education. Changes in general education—and the implications for institutions grappling with those changes—are the heart of this book, which looks at how higher education institutions have designed and carried out such reforms and the lessons that can be learned from their experiences.

"General education" here means the organized set of activities designed to promote critical-thinking and writing skills, knowledge of the liberal arts, and personal and social responsibilities. Stated in the broadest terms, general education is that part of the curriculum that teaches both civic responsibility and the value of arts, sciences, and humanities. In an era of increasing specialization general education is often seen as a corrective for the narrow concentration of a professional or occupational curriculum, providing both a common core of knowledge and a breadth of knowledge and skills.

The ostensible focus of reform in general education is, of course, on what students are learning—or not learning, as the case may be. Except for teaching writing skills, however, there is little agreement on the specifics of general education. Western civilization, multiculturalism, civics—all have had their advocates. Many recent works have dealt with the topic of student learning, on why and how it should be reformed. In contrast, only a few have examined how those reforms are taking place, who is involved, and how the reforms affect institutions, their administrators, and their faculties.

This book fills that gap. It turns its lens not on the effect of reform on students but on the reform process itself—its catalysts and its effects on the institutions engaged in the struggle to provide their students with the fundamentals of a liberal arts education. The book is intended for higher education policy makers, researchers, and administrators, especially those in the many institutions that have undertaken or are about to undertake similar curricular changes. It is also aimed at faculty and students interested in organizational change, in policy studies, and in higher education generally. It should appeal as well to readers interested in the fate of academic values at higher education institutions and in the preparation of a democratic citizenry. In short, the book is for anyone who wants a better understanding of the complexities of curricular change on campuses and of the effects—anticipated and unanticipated—on academic structure and processes. As just one example of these effects, changes and reforms in general education requirements often dramatically alter students' course-taking patterns, thereby affecting the status and size of departments. Thus, for faculty in their departments the ideal of creating a proper foundation for student learning is sometimes at odds with a more immediate concern for economic survival.

Among the questions forming the foundation of this analysis are the following:

- What brings a campus to the point of wanting to change its general education curriculum?
- Is the process of change as rational and planned as the current literature makes it appear, or do organizational constraints and nonrational elements influence the outcome? If so, to what extent?
- What are some common impediments to curricular change, and how can they be avoided?
- How and to what extent do outside forces influence curricular reform?
- What is the interplay of culture and politics in the process of changing the general education curriculum?

RESEARCH APPROACH

This book is one of the outcomes of a study conducted by the New England Resource Center for Higher Education, at the Graduate College of Education, University of Massachusetts Boston, of how colleges and universities have instituted and carried out changes in their general education programs. Most writing about the curriculum tends not to be based on empirical research into what actually happens on campuses. Empirical research into campus issues relies primarily on mail questionnaires (American Council on Education, 1988, 1992, 1994; Gaff, 1983, 1991). Important though these surveys may be, it is not clear who fills out the questionnaires, although they are usually addressed to an administrator. Because they do not usually provide a context from which to understand responses, the accuracy of such surveys is difficult to evaluate and may include a bias toward administrative perspectives.

This book takes a broader approach to the study of general education and curricular reform. Rather than relying on a mail survey, it draws upon a telephone survey in which it is clear who the respondent is and which allows for the kind of exploration and clarification that is impossible in a mail questionnaire. In addition to the telephone survey the book draws upon case studies of campuses where efforts were made to change general education. The case studies are built from interviews with a variety of administrators, past and present, and with faculty from various disciplines and at all ranks. The telephone surveys and campus visits provide multiple perspectives and a context for understanding these perspectives (see Appendix A).

The Sample

The colleges and universities in the sample range in size from large, regional institutions offering graduate and undergraduate programs to small, local institutions offering only undergraduate degrees. The sample does not include relatively well-off liberal arts colleges and research universities, community colleges, or technical colleges.

Much has been written about the undergraduate curriculum in prestigious doctorate-granting institutions and selective liberal arts colleges, whereas little has been written about the schools that have long been at the barricades, making prodigious efforts to improve the liberal arts curriculum despite severely limited resources, great demands on their faculties, and student bodies that are academically less talented than those of more selective institutions.

Nevertheless, the findings of this study may apply with equal force to the better-known institutions. Over the past decade these colleges and universities have become increasingly subject to the same kinds of pressures that earlier affected less well-endowed institutions. Pressed to modify long-standing curricula to keep up to date and struggling to meet ever rising costs with diminishing resources (or diminishing rates of growth in those resources), the more selective institutions are confronting the same questions that less selective institutions have been dealing with for more than a decade.

Telephone Interviews

The study took place in two stages. In the first stage, 71 telephone interviews were conducted at institutions of higher education in New England, with senior academic officers or someone they designated as especially knowledgeable (see Appendix B for list of institutions). The telephone interviews focused on identifying when the institution last changed its general education requirements, how extensive those changes were, how long it took to implement them, and what resources were used for this purpose (see Appendix C for questionnaire). Respondents were given the opportunity to introduce elements of their own and to interject their own analyses of general education and the change process.

Campus Visits

On the basis of findings from the telephone survey, the research team selected 12 institutions for intensive campus visits; the team also conducted campus visits outside New England at three institutions recommended by nationally recognized curriculum experts as having exemplary general education programs. Teams of two or three researchers visited each of the 15 institutions, conducting face-to-face interviews with administrators, faculty, and staff identified as active at some point in planning or implementing the new general education program. The teams conducted a total of 235 such interviews in the period 1989–1992. Free-ranging and complex, the interviews focused on the source of the change in the general education program; how various individuals and committees conducted their business; points of agreement and contention, support and opposition; the role of the faculty and the administration in the changes; and implementation of the reforms (see Appendix B for a profile of the 15 institutions and Appendix D for the questionnaire used in these personal interviews).

In addition to reporting on the results of these surveys, the book includes brief portraits of the institutions visited, highlighting their experiences in carrying out reforms of general education. These portraits, although accurately representing the events that took place, do not identify specific individuals who took part in the events. In the interests of preserving confidentiality, identifying characteristics of participants in a few cases have been changed to protect their identity.

PERSPECTIVES ON CHANGE

Changes in the general education curriculum cannot be understood without carefully considering all the elements that give such changes life—the differing perspectives of administrators and faculty members; campus values and collective arrangements; the joining of events and circumstances, both local and national; and the program itself. In this book, curriculum development is explored in a way that includes the most engaging and the most human kinds of behavior. This focus on people and their circumstances, including but not limited to their commitments to intellectual ideals regarding the content and role of the curriculum, reveals foible as well as virtue, happenstance as well as calculated plan. Running parallel to the official project of curriculum change are other issues, subtexts that can profoundly influence the nature and extent of that change. These subtexts include the relationships among established organizational units and general education as a way of maintaining or increasing departmental enrollments, as a way of saving faculty jobs, and as a means of giving an admissions department a program it can promote. Another type of issue that enters the general education design and implementation process is less obvious, involving struggles for power far less dependent on the traditional campus units of organization, such as the emergence of new voices among the faculty. The framework for this book thus makes room for what is seldom seen—the nonrational, unplanned, and even unwanted aspects of organizational change. These aspects almost always accompany change but to date are unreported in the literature on general education.

The book examines the more rational elements of change as well. The chapters view curricular and organizational reform through various perspectives, from historical and socioeconomic to cultural and political, exploring in the conclusions the practical implications of the research and distilling lessons for strategies of general education change. This does not necessarily mean that any one of the institutions reported on should be held up as a model of "best practices." What worked in one place may not work in others. Furthermore, faculty, administrators, and staff in these colleges and universities could easily describe the imperfections, flaws, and mistakes in the change process; some were eager to do so. Equally apparent, however, these institutions had done much correctly and, in some cases, they were astonishingly ingenious and perspicacious.

Thus what is present in this book are ideals and models of change that reformers can adapt to local circumstance. If these analyses of the experience of institutions save even a few campuses from making unnecessary mistakes—especially those that cause great campus division—the effort will have been successful. An even better measure of success will be whether more intelligent, mature, and effective reform processes result in curricula that allow faculty, administrators, and, most of all, students to grow and to learn.

▶ 1

The Precarious State of General Education

*Many institutions now are trying to regain
public trust by devoting increased energy and
resources to improving the quality and effi-
ciency of undergraduate education.*
—*DAVID W. BRENEMAN (1995, p. 111)*

Since 1977, when the Carnegie Foundation for the Advancement of Teaching declared general education a "disaster area,"
higher education institutions and the national media have focused on the problem. The fate of the liberal arts and general
education—that part of the curriculum intended to convey the
value of arts, sciences, and the humanities along with civic
responsibility—has become a continuing concern. Foundations
and federal agencies have sponsored a variety of projects, and
higher education associations have organized conferences on
the undergraduate curriculum. At liberal arts colleges, research
universities, community colleges, and state colleges an old
question persists: "What should every educated person know?"
This book looks at how U.S. colleges and universities have tried

1

to answer that question, at their struggle to improve general education, and at the aftermath.

Our focus is on colleges and universities that are neither famous nor wealthy, with students who are typically the first in their families to go to college. These institutions came into their own after World War II, during the great shift from elite to mass higher education (Riesman, Gusfield, & Gamson, 1970). Even in the expansionary period of the 1960s and 1970s they were classic resource-dependent organizations, with little self-sufficiency, subject to unpredictable shifts in the market and in state policies (Pfeffer & Salancik, 1978). Some are denigrated as "local Podunks" with tenuous claims on the term "college" or "university." Histories of higher education tend to ignore them in favor of the older, more influential, nationally known liberal arts colleges and research universities. Contemporary accounts of these institutions usually focus on striking cases like Alverno College in Milwaukee, Wisconsin or Evergreen State College in Olympia, Washington—schools known for their unique curricula. However, the language used to describe the vast majority of these schools emphasizes that they are nonelite, unselective, neither research institutions nor true liberal arts colleges. In short, the emphasis is on what they are not (Birnbaum, 1985; Breneman, 1990, 1994).[1]

Why study them? Because they are where the masses of students are enrolled. In 1994, such institutions constituted almost 70 percent of the general four-year colleges and universities in the United States, enrolling almost 50 percent of the students in four-year institutions (Carnegie Foundation for the Advancement of Teaching, 1994).

Some hold that academic values and mass education are contradictory, that the general run of first-generation college students is unprepared for or uninterested in liberal learning (Traub, 1994). Yet many nonselective schools have gone to extraordinary lengths to strengthen general education, which is devoted to the preparation of a democratic citizenry (Gamson & Associates, 1984; Kimball, 1986; Steiner, 1994; Weaver, 1991).

Their efforts say much about the promise of democracy in the last decade of the 20th century, and the contribution of higher education to that promise, much more than the "core curriculum" debates at Harvard or the disputes over the canon at Stanford (Carnochan, 1993; Keller, 1982). These institutions are responsible for the intellectual preparation of the Americans who are the backbone of the labor force and of their communities, those citizens who make up the families of "middle America."

LIFE ON A ROLLER COASTER

Like all of higher education, the colleges and universities serving middle America were profoundly shaped by the arrival of the baby-boom generation after World War II. The GI Bill, tuition dollars from families who benefited from an expanding economy, and federal and state student-aid programs led to larger student bodies (Birnbaum, 1985; Dunham, 1969; Pfnister, 1984, 1985).[2] Not only did these private "invisible colleges" (Astin & Lee, 1972) and public colleges of the "forgotten Americans" (Dunham, 1969) increase their enrollments in a short time, but new colleges and universities were established, later to be absorbed along with older institutions into the growing state systems across the country. Faculty work conditions were improved, and buildings were added. As ever more tuition dollars and government support materialized for these resource-starved institutions, they broadened their offerings and their student bodies. In the process many of them lost their once distinctive religious, racial, gender, or curricular character (Finnegan & Gamson, 1996).[3]

Shifts in institutional mission were accompanied by other changes. Labor-market shortages in the early to middle 1960s put faculty in a better bargaining position than earlier generations of faculty had held, leading to an increase in faculty power. The movement to a buyers' market in the late 1960s, when there was an oversupply of Ph.D.'s, paradoxically reinforced faculty power by bringing in more faculty with doctorates, many from prestigious universities. Most of the new faculty were committed to scholarly work and to pointing their institutions in a cosmopolitan, intellectually serious direction. As time passed, they and their allies, often senior administrators, transformed the culture of their institutions.

During this period higher education assimilated distinctive and local cultures into a national model based on prestigious colleges and universities. This national model prizes loyalty to a discipline or professional field rather than to an institution, high mobility, and personal visibility, all based on a political economy fueled by research and publication. Several forces were responsible for this change. Federal funding for colleges and universities introduced common regulatory requirements. Higher education publications, such as *The Chronicle of Higher Education* and *Change* magazine, as well as the many national associations and foundations for higher education, defined an agenda for higher education as a whole (Gamson, 1987). In contrast to earlier times, when presidents and deans were recruited from within the faculty or from circles that had historically supported these institutions, more and more institutions brought in senior administrators from nationwide sources, people already aware of or engaged in the national discourse about higher education (McLaughlin & Riesman, 1990). With recently hired faculty these institutions began looking outward for prestigious models they could emulate. In sociological terms, they were on a quest for prestige based on imitating successful institutions (DiMaggio & Powell, 1983).

Then the roller coaster plunged. In the early 1970s the job market for college graduates took a turn for the worse as the economy declined. By the mid-1970s, competition for students increased. At the same time, most colleges and universities experienced a decline in student preparation,[4] which, in the institutions serving middle America, had never been high in any case (Astin & Lee, 1972; Birnbaum, 1985). In 1976, students in less selective colleges and universities had the lowest grade-point averages among students in four-year institutions (Carnegie Foundation, 1977).

The less selective schools always had to appeal to the practical, security-oriented needs of a large group of first-generation students. These needs were especially urgent in a declining economy. In *Missions of the College Curriculum* the Carnegie Foundation for the Advancement of Teaching (1977) reported that students in less selective institutions were more likely than students in other four-year institutions to say they would drop out of college if attending college did not improve their job chances. Between 65 and 70 percent of the students in these institutions said that getting training and skills for an occupation was essential, compared with 36 percent of the students in leading liberal arts colleges.

VULNERABILITY AND RETRENCHMENT

Just as the costs of responding to students' needs for professional and academic preparation were rising, support from the federal government and the states began leveling off and even declining.[5] This combination of circumstances hit private, nonelite institutions with great force (Chaffee, 1984; Hammond, 1984). After years of moving away from their old missions they could no longer count on the loyalty of traditional supporters, nor could they compete on costs with state colleges and universities, which they came to resemble (Finkelstein, Farrar, & Pfnister, 1984; Pfnister, 1985).[6] Internally faculty became more fractured by the entry of Ph.D.'s from prestigious universities, and splits between faculty and administration became more pronounced, partly because faculty expected that lower teaching loads and more support for research would materialize (which did not happen) and partly because administrators sometimes used these schools as stepping-stones to more prestigious institutions.

As the years passed, these institutions became increasingly vulnerable. Some even had to close.[7] The survivors had little security, however. The Carnegie Council on Policy Studies in Higher Education (1980) issued a widely cited warning about their vulnerability:

> It is not generally possible for them to greatly lower their admission requirements, and they usually recruit in their localities. For the latter reason, they can be badly affected if they are in a small town or rural area that is losing population or in a state that is losing population. . . . They can also be vulnerable if they are in a large metropolitan area with a vast range of low-tuition public institutions. (p. 60)

Larger institutions—especially public ones—with their more diverse portfolios of programs could weather the storm more easily (Birnbaum, 1985). In a few years, however, they too were battered by reductions in state support.[8] By the 1990s few institutions remained immune to the financial pressures created by these shifts in support.

Like many other higher education institutions, the less selective colleges and universities have responded to the situation first by retrenching faculty and then by restructuring academic programs and personnel policies. When students prefer vocational preparation and spurn the liberal arts, colleges refocus on applied programs. Arts and sciences departments scramble to offer courses that will appeal to career interests, although few have succeeded in luring the students back. Professional programs, often overresponding to escalating requirements from professional accrediting associations, resist general education requirements that add to their students' burdens. The result is that most uncommitted resources, including faculty positions, have been shifted to professional programs and colleges in business, communication, nursing, and engineering (see Figure 1–1) and to remedial programs.

Percent

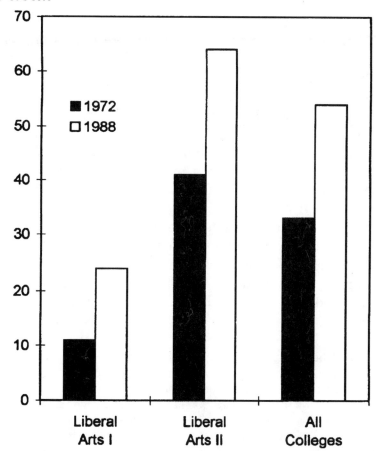

FIGURE 1-1 Professional Degrees Awarded by Liberal Arts Colleges, 1972, 1988

From *Liberal Arts Colleges: Thriving, Surviving, or Endangered?* (Appendix A, Figure A-1, p. 140; and p. 11) by David W. Breneman, 1994, Washington, D.C.: The Brookings Institution. Author's calculations based on data from the National Center for Higher Education Systems, Boulder, Colorado. Reprinted by permission of The Brookings Institution.

The 1987 Carnegie Foundation for the Advancement of Teaching classification of institutions of higher education divided 540 private liberal arts colleges into two groups: 140 liberal arts I colleges and 400 liberal arts II colleges. The highly selective liberal arts I institutions are primarily undergraduate colleges that award more than half of their baccalaureate degrees in arts and science fields.

Liberal arts II colleges are primarily undergraduate colleges that are less selective and award more than half of their degrees in liberal arts fields. This category also includes a group of colleges that award *less* than half of their degrees in liberal arts fields but, with fewer than 1,500 students, are too small to be considered comprehensive.

7

In the growing competition for scarce resources in their institutions, liberal arts departments are the losers. An analysis of changes in the shares of baccalaureate degrees conferred between 1954 and 1986 (Turner & Bowen, 1990) showed that arts and science degrees increased by 11.7 percent between 1954 and 1970 but decreased by 17.7 percent between 1970 and 1986. Relationships between arts and sciences and professional programs have grown increasingly conflictual, although neither camp has much internal cohesion (Wilshire, 1990).

Fewer and fewer students have been majoring in the traditional liberal arts disciplines, transforming many of the less selective liberal arts colleges, if they have grown large enough, into comprehensive institutions.[9] Those that remained small have changed in ways that led David Breneman (1990) to declare:

> While I began [my research] with the belief that there were roughly 600 [private liberal arts colleges] in this country, I have concluded that, given a reasonable definition of a liberal arts college, we have only about 200 of them left. . . . The liberal arts college as we know it is disappearing from the landscape, and another type of institution—the professional college—is taking its place. (p. 17)

NATIONAL GENERAL EDUCATION MOVEMENT

A new cycle of attention to general education, the most recent of several that have occurred throughout this century, made its appearance in the early 1980s (Rudolph, 1977; Thatcher, 1991), prompted in part by the Carnegie Foundation's assessment in *Missions of the College Curriculum* (1977):

> The erosion of general education on America's college campuses is even more severe than its share of curricula might indicate. . . .

We believe that the general education idea continues to have a place in American colleges and universities. We would hope that colleges could make greater efforts to define it and set limits on the extent to which further erosion will be permitted. (p. 184)

With support from several private foundations and federal agencies, national associations have initiated studies and special projects to improve general and liberal education (Association of American Colleges, 1985; Bennett, 1984; Gaff, 1983; Gamson & Associates, 1984; Rockefeller Foundation, 1979; Study Group on the Conditions of Excellence in American Higher Education, 1984; Weaver, 1991; Wuest, 1979). The overriding message delivered by reports of these groups resonates with the recent history of higher education: The undergraduate curriculum has lost its liberal arts roots. Students lack exposure to fundamental subjects and are not acquiring basic intellectual skills.[10]

The Carnegie Foundation report captured a deep dissatisfaction with general education among faculty around the country. A national survey published a year after the Carnegie report showed that half of the faculty favored some sort of core curriculum (Levine, 1978). The currency of the term "core curriculum" in the 1990s expresses at once the reach for coherence, for rigor, and for intellectual community among college faculties. Specialists in different disciplines are talking with one another, often for the first time in their professional lives, about their fields and why they care about them. Traditionalists and innovators, humanists and scientists, teachers and administrators are meeting about the curriculum. Educators with an interest in adapting new programs from the previous two decades, such as women's studies and ethnic studies, are sparring with proponents of Western culture. Faculty who talk about competencies, critical thinking, writing across the curriculum, quantitative reasoning, and computer literacy are introducing skills into the repertoire of curriculum reformers (Gaff, 1983; Gamson & Associates, 1984; Grant, 1979).

New programs and courses are being invented, and expertise is available to help put them in place (Gaff, 1983; Gamson & Associates, 1984; Levine, 1978). Certain programs receive special attention. In 1984, Secretary of Education William Bennett cited (1984) the core curricula at Saint Joseph's College in Indiana and at Brooklyn College in New York. Brooklyn College in the early 1980s decided that all students would be required to take a basic core of 10 courses, an updated version of a core curriculum it had abandoned in the previous decade. Harvard College, in a celebrated move, introduced its own version of a core curriculum (Keller, 1982). Colleges and universities across the country are keenly aware of these models.

In some of the universities built around a teachers college or other professional school, where there has never been a strong liberal arts tradition, the question of what every educated person should know is being pondered seriously for the first time. The new national general education movement has strengthened the position of liberal arts faculty. By now almost all colleges and universities in the country have climbed onto the bandwagon (American Council on Education, 1988).

They are doing so at an inauspicious time. The search for students and resources in higher education is endless and increasingly bleak. In the late 1980s the national economy began a downturn that was traumatic to many nonelite institutions, whose experience has generalized to all of higher education in the 1990s. After a period of relative security even well-known private institutions, such as Bennington College, face serious threats to their survival, and public institutions, such as the University of California and the State University of New York, confront continuing degradation because of unpredictable and deep cutbacks in state support. Poor academic preparation and worries about getting jobs drive even upper-middle-class students away from the liberal arts. The struggle to revitalize general education continues unabated.

NOTES

1. Two types of higher education institutions are the focus of this book: what the Carnegie Foundation for the Advancement of Teaching, in *A Classification of Institutions of Higher Education* (1994), identified as (1) "master's (comprehensive) colleges and universities"—institutions offering "a full range of baccalaureate programs and . . . graduate education through the master's degree"—and (2) "baccalaureate (liberal arts) colleges II"—"primarily undergraduate colleges [that emphasize] baccalaureate-degree programs, [that] are less restrictive in admissions [than liberal arts colleges I, and that typically] award less than 40 percent of their . . . degrees in liberal arts fields." The master's institutions are further broken down into categories I and II. Master's I institutions award 40 or more master's degrees annually in three or more disciplines; master's II institutions award 20 or more master's degrees annually in one or more disciplines. (See Appendix A for a description of the other Carnegie categories.) Aside from differences in size, the master's institutions and baccalaureate colleges II resemble each other in their precariousness and in their mix of liberal arts and professional emphases.

2. For example, total undergraduate enrollment more than doubled in less than a decade between 1963 and 1970, from 3.6 million to 7.4 million. In the same period the enrollment of students in two-year institutions increased from 0.6 million to 2.2 million. See U.S. Department of Health, Education and Welfare (1963) and Kenneth A. Simon and W. Vance Grant (1973).

3. The master's (comprehensive) institutions had diverse beginnings (Finnegan & Gamson, 1996). Most were established in the 19th century—a few in the 18th—and most began as normal schools to prepare schoolteachers in primary subjects (Finnegan, 1991). During the second half of the 19th century they offered other specialized technical training in agricultural and mechanical, technical, and business institutions, including urban evening schools founded by the Young Men's Christian Association (YMCA).

Another large group of master's institutions began like many of the colleges classified as baccalaureate (liberal arts) colleges II (Astin & Lee, 1972; Pfnister, 1985). These institutions include those with Roman Catholic and Protestant roots that began as seminaries, Bible colleges, or liberal arts colleges for students of a particular faith. Several historically black colleges, most with a strong emphasis on vocational curricula, began after the Civil War as church-related schools or as land-grant institutions.

For whatever reason—an unappealing location, a limited constituency, poor leadership—these baccalaureate colleges II never became national institutions like the baccalaureate colleges I with similar beginnings. Some remained small colleges with small student bodies and limited curricular offerings. Others grew larger, evolving into master's (comprehensive) institutions. The colleges and universities established in the 20th century were likely to develop into master's institutions. These evolved from junior colleges (some were women's colleges)—extensions and branches of existing universities and of full-fledged state colleges and universities (Finnegan, 1991).

4. Between 1970 and 1980, Scholastic Aptitude Test (SAT) scores for college-bound high school seniors declined from an average of 948 to 890. See Thomas D. Snyder and Charlene M. Hoffman (1994).

5. For example, federal and state support constituted 12.2 percent of the total current fund revenue of independent institutions in 1964; by 1990 it had declined to 6.7 percent, and it dropped to even lower levels in the interim years of 1970 (5.1 percent) and 1980 (1.4 percent). See Kenneth A. Simon and W. Vance Grant (1973), W. Vance Grant and Leo J. Eiden (1982), and Thomas D. Snyder and Charlene M. Hoffman (1994).

6. The categories are not, however, mutually exclusive. Some of the larger nonelite institutions in the study are state universities, and some liberal arts colleges in the study are state colleges.

7. Among a total of 107 closures of colleges and universities from 1970 to 1978, two fifths were less selective liberal arts colleges. In a total of 68 mergers during the same period, more than a quarter involved these liberal arts institutions. See Carnegie Council on Policy Studies in Higher Education, *Three Thousand Futures* (1980), calculations based on table D-3, pp. 211–212.

8. Although in absolute dollars both state and federal support of public institutions has risen in the last three decades, between 1980 and 1990 state support as a proportion of the total current fund revenue of public institutions declined from 30.7 percent to 26.5 percent. In the same period federal support for public institutions declined as a proportion of the total, from 8.7 (1980) to 6.6 percent (1990). See Kenneth A. Simon and W. Vance Grant (1973); W. Vance Grant and Leo J. Eiden (1982); Thomas D. Snyder and Charlene M. Hoffman (1994).

9. Joan Gilbert (1995) argued that the decline in the proportion of liberal arts degrees is not a short-term but a long-term trend, present for at least a century, with interruptions in the 1950s and 1960s. She also noted the existence, since 1985, of "renewed interest in the liberal arts, although it has occurred primarily outside liberal arts colleges, in larger institutions with PhD programs" (p. 37). See "The Liberal Arts College— Is It Really an Endangered Species?" *Change* (Sept./Oct.), 37–43.

10. A study by Clifford Adelman (1994) tracked more than 5,000 students from the graduating high school class of 1972 who had earned bachelor's degrees between 1972 and 1984. He found, for example, that among recipients of the bachelor's degree almost three out of five (58.4 percent) had earned no college credits in foreign languages; two out of five (39.6 percent) had earned no credits in English and American literature; and one out of four (26.2 percent) had earned no credits in history. As might be expected, many of those who lacked credits in such courses were preparing for technical careers. However, even among education majors, for example, the lack of exposure to cultural studies was extremely high: 31.1 percent had no credits in English and American literature and 71.1 percent had no credits in foreign languages. As Adelman pointed out, "Culture takes a back seat in college" (p. 201). See *Lessons of a Generation: Education and Work in the Lives of the High School Class of 1972* (1994), tables 5.2, 5.3, 5.4, and 5.5.

▶ 2

The Push and Pull of the Outside

Ideally, the twin obligations of institutional integrity and public accountability can be kept in balance. In practice, pressures seem continuously to push the campus in one direction, then another.
—*CARNEGIE FOUNDATION FOR THE ADVANCEMENT OF TEACHING (1982, p. 3)*

Higher education has weathered crises before. In the 20th century alone, U.S. colleges and universities have lived through a major depression, recessions, two world wars, a presidential assassination, the civil rights movement, draft protests, and demands for sexual equality. Through each circumstance they remained relatively autonomous, free to attend to their educational responsibilities. The current crisis, however, involves college and universities more directly. Educational institutions no longer have the luxury of being bystanders; now, more than ever, public criticism is directed at colleges and universities. There is a perception that postsecondary institutions are insular and self-serving, that they are not doing enough to solve society's economic and social ills. State governments have reacted to these criticisms with a host of laws and policies regulating colleges and universities. To add to the turmoil, precarious economic conditions and a declining pool of 18- to 20-year-olds have created a financial crisis for many public and private colleges and universities. Although few institutions have closed, many have changed the way they operate.

Drawing upon interviews from campus visits, this chapter explores how increasing interdependence between higher education and political and social forces, combined with economic instability, has changed the campus climate and affected the impetus to reform general education. To what extent is social and political interdependence a threat to the autonomy of colleges and universities? That question has long concerned observers of higher education. More than a decade ago the Carnegie Foundation for the Advancement of Teaching issued *The Control of the Campus* (1982), a report about the governance of higher education that focused, in part, on the tensions inherent in the relationship between government and postsecondary education.

> At times, excessive demands of society chip away at the integrity of the university. At other times, the academy seems unresponsive to public needs. . . . How can colleges and universities that are increasingly in the nation's service sustain their traditions of self-control while being accountable to the various constituencies they serve? (pp. 3–4)

The report depicted campus governance structures as having been weakened by their increasing need to respond to outside forces. Unless changes were made to strengthen self-regulation, the authors warned, the locus of power over colleges and universities would surely shift to outside institutions. Faculty and administrators would lose their ability to govern their institutions and the quality of educational programs would be compromised. Since the publication of the 1982 Carnegie report, outside agencies, especially at the state level, have significantly increased their power over colleges and universities. Although day-to-day management remains the domain of campus administrators, state coordinating agencies now routinely demand that colleges and universities justify their operations in order to receive state funds or introduce new programs (Hines, 1988). Interdependence threatens the management of colleges and universities because external agencies, especially those in the political sector, have both the authority and the resources to dictate the terms by which those institutions function.

ORGANIZATIONAL ENVIRONMENT

Not all institutions are equally vulnerable to outside pressures. Clark Kerr (1991) wrote that higher education's elite institutions—independent private universities, such as Harvard and Yale—are more buffered from outside forces. Independent public institutions—independent in ownership and financing but dependent in control, such as the University of Michigan— are slightly less autonomous. Kerr ranked semi-independent public colleges and universities—publicly controlled institutions with some degree of self-sustaining financial support, such as the University of Vermont—third in his scale. He ranked "dependent" private and public institutions as least autonomous. Dependent private colleges have lay boards of trustees, and their revenue comes almost entirely from tuition fees. Dependent public colleges and universities rely almost completely upon the state for their operations. These schools include all of the institutions visited as part of this research and most of the institutions that were part of the initial telephone survey.

Kerr's classification of degrees of autonomy is helpful. Howard E. Aldrich's *Organizations and Environment* (1979), a landmark book, further illuminated the causes and effects of institutional dependency. In Aldrich's view, the immutability of an organization's boundaries and its ability to control the entry and exit of its members are the hallmarks of its autonomy. These abilities depend, in turn, upon the organization's internal needs and the degree of threat posed by the organization's environment. The description of environmental conditions that follows is based on Aldrich's complex analysis.

Four characteristics of the environment of higher education institutions are especially important for an analysis of their autonomy: decreasing and unstable resources, increasing competition among colleges and universities, declining student enrollment, and increasing external influences and control. Because declining enrollment is inevitably linked to increased competition, the two factors are discussed as a single category labeled the declining market for students.

Decreasing and Unstable Resources

The federal government has never been a generous contributor to the revenues of colleges and universities. By the 1980s federal monies accounted for just 8 percent of the net revenues of public colleges and universities and less than 2 percent of revenues for private colleges and universities (Hoenack & Collins, 1990). For most of the last 30 years, state and local funds for higher education have grown (American Council on Education, 1989), notwithstanding a series of cyclical downturns in the 1950s and 1960s, which brought about a temporary decline. During the 1980s, however, states began to reduce the percentage of their budgets earmarked for higher education. In 1980, states allocated 8.3 percent of their tax dollars to higher education. By 1989 this percentage had dropped to 7.2 percent. Two years later, in the midst of a recession, state contributions fell to 6.9 percent (Barrow, 1993).

For some states, especially those in the Northeast and Midwest, the economic bubble burst in the 1980s. A severe recession led to sharp cuts in state spending as revenues declined precipitously. Between 1979 and 1985, 28 states and the District of Columbia reduced their subsidies per full-time enrolled (FTE) student to offset declines in public funds, some by as much as one third of the total higher education appropriation (Hoenack & Collins, 1990).

Since 1980, tuition charges have risen faster than the rate of inflation. Private colleges began to increase tuition in the early 1980s to offset increasing costs and slowly growing federal student aid. On average, public colleges and universities increased tuition even more to compensate for a loss in public funds (Zumeta, 1995). In only a few states did rising tuition offset the decline in state revenues (Hoenack & Collins, 1990).

Declining Market for Students

The college experience is, among other things, a product bought and sold in the marketplace. Colleges and universities attract students by a combination of competitive prices (tuition) and differentiated quality of goods (course offerings, programs, faculty, student services, etc.). Successful differentiation can produce, in economic terms, control over a segment of the marketplace. In Aldrich's terms, marketplace control can be translated into the ability to control the entry and exit of students. In reality, however, most educational institutions—with the possible exception of the most selective—have limited power in the marketplace. Because they are seldom informed about what kinds of price and quality adjustments their competitors are making to attract students, they are uncertain about which educational strategies to pursue. Furthermore, potential students have different ways of assessing the relative value of different mixes of educational prices and products.

By the late 1970s higher education officials began making plans to cope with the expected decline in the college-age population (American Council on Education, 1989). With forecasts of enrollment declines of 15 to 20 percent in the 1980s and beyond, observers expected major shake-ups. Books and conferences devoted to managing the decline became fashionable as institutions scrambled to gain comparative advantage. Dependent colleges and universities had good reason to fear the decline, relying as they did almost entirely upon student tuition for operational funds. Public dependent colleges and universities also had cause to worry. State practice often linked the size of campus budgets to student enrollments—the more students, the larger the budget. Even where state practice differed, many public higher education administrators were and remain convinced that state appropriations decline in the face of decreased enrollment (Leslie et al., 1990).

Increasing External Influences and Control

Federal involvement in higher education has largely been limited to increasing equality of educational opportunity and sponsoring basic research and development. Historically, with the exceptions of subsidizing land-grant colleges in the Morrill Federal Land Grant Act of 1862, enforcing antidiscrimination measures of the Civil Rights Act of 1964, and providing student aid, beginning with the Higher Education Act of 1965, the federal government has taken a laissez-faire stance toward the governance of higher education (Keppel, 1987; Rudolph, 1962).

In contrast, the states have a long history of involvement in the governance of higher education. Among the provisions of the federal higher education amendments of 1972 are Section 1202 on the State Postsecondary Education Commission, which was intended to increase state higher education planning and coordination, and Section 1203, which authorized funds for statewide planning. State planning commissions now provide oversight for a host of programs and policies, including state student-aid programs, admission requirements to public colleges and universities, and, most recently, program review and assessment. By 1987, for example, two thirds of the states had initiated state assessment procedures to evaluate student and institutional performance. About two thirds of state higher education boards viewed their role as either actively encouraging institutions to enact assessment procedures or initiating such procedures themselves (Hines, 1988).

State political officials, among others, view colleges and universities as more than places where students acquire knowledge. They are also seen as agencies that serve the public interest. In return for financial assistance, they are expected to advance the social and economic aims of the state. During the recessionary period of the late 1980s, for example, when governors and state legislators in the Northeast focused their energies on programs that would restore their states' economic health, discussion about the link between education and prosperity abounded. State officials pressured institutions to play stronger roles in economic development, especially in educating students to be productive workers. Officials valued colleges and universities for their ability to service the states' vocational needs and judged institutions on their ability to train employable workers (Fairweather, 1989; Pew Higher Education Roundtable, 1994).

A more significant form of intervention has come from the six regional accrediting agencies across the country. Members are the colleges and universities in each region. These agencies are self-regulating; member colleges and universities formulate a set of standards for the measurement of student learning and create a system for assessing the educational quality of member schools. The common practice is for an institution to undertake a self-study, which is then reviewed in a campus visit by a team of volunteers from other accredited institutions. The team makes recommendations to a commission, which has the final say.

Accreditation provides respectability and assurance of a minimum standard of quality; its absence means that students attending a member college are ineligible for federal student aid and loans. In recent years, accreditors have focused attention on issues of institutional quality and student achievement (National Policy Board of Higher Education Institutional Accreditation, 1994). This increased scrutiny has been directed at making sure that institutions meet or exceed appropriate undergraduate academic standards.

CAMPUS RESPONSES

As shown in Table 2–1, four campuses where campus visits were conducted had experienced all three of the environmental conditions—decreasing and unstable resources, a declining market for students, and increasing external influences and control. Three campuses reported experiencing two conditions, and six reported one condition. Only two campuses indicated no outside influences just before or during the period of general education reform. Responses to these environmental factors have depended largely upon unique conditions on campuses. However, three general strategies have emerged: cutting costs, becoming more competitive, and accelerating responses to market changes.

Cutting Costs

When revenues decline, administrators cut costs. Faculty salaries and benefits are at the center of most cost-cutting strategies. In almost all the private institutions visited, action had been taken to freeze or withdraw faculty positions and salaries and to increase faculty workload. Often a single administrator, usually the chief executive officer, made the decision to cut costs; deans and provosts carried out the decision. One of the first official acts of a new dean on one campus in the study, for instance, was to reduce the college budget by 10 percent and the faculty by 20 percent. During the same period in the early 1980s a private college replaced tenure with contracts of varying lengths of time. One president postponed all tenure decisions until the college was on better economic footing. Untenured faculty were no longer assured employment; on several campuses the decision to rehire faculty was based upon

TABLE 2–1   Influence of Environment on Campuses Visited

College/ University	Year GE Discussion Began	Environmental Influences Just Before or During Period of GE Design	Campus Actions Just Before or During Period of GE Design
Albertus Magnus	1976	Enrollment decline Revenue decline	Became coeducational Imposed 5-year moratorium on tenure Froze salaries
Bridgeport, Univ. of	1976	Enrollment decline Heavy debt	Cut back faculty Faculty unionized
Bridgewater State	1983	None	None
Colby-Sawyer	1982	Accreditation visit Enrollment decline Revenue decline	Cut back faculty Froze salaries
Green Mountain	1985	Critical GE comments on accreditation report Enrollment decline Revenue decline	Cut back faculty Froze salaries Expanded liberal arts majors
Hartford, Univ. of	1985	State board of education mandate that one third of curriculum be GE	None
Johnson State	1981	Enrollment decline Budget cutbacks Elimination of duplicative majors by system board	None
Kean	1980	Revision by state board of B.A. requirements Accreditation visit	None
Maine, Univ. of, at Machias	1980	Requirement of system office for campus long-range plan	None
Massachusetts, Univ. of, Boston	1977	Budget cutbacks	Merged two colleges
Minnesota, Univ. of, Morris	1985	System president's report urging campuses to specialize Revenue decline	Campus differentiated its curriculum from that of the flagship university

(Continued)

TABLE 2–1   *(Continued)*

College/ University	Year GE Discussion Began	Environmental Influences Just Before or During Period of GE Design	Campus Actions Just Before or During Period of GE Design
New England	1987	Critical GE comments on accreditation report Enrollment decline Revenue decline	Expanded vocational offerings Cut back faculty Froze salaries
Plymouth State	1983	Critical GE comments on accreditation report	None
Roger Williams	1985	Accreditation visit	None
Seattle University	1980	None	None

B.A. = bachelor of arts; GE = general education

short-term need. At one college, faculty had to wait until late spring before receiving offers to teach in the following academic year. The offers were made only after students had committed themselves to attending the college. Even then the college refused to make salary decisions until fall, when it would have firm enrollment numbers.

In response to fiscal difficulties some private institutions have let faculty go. Inevitably the stories of departures are told and retold until, years after the event, they take on mythical proportions. At New England College the saga was told of a handful of faculty who left the college in the early 1980s. That several had left voluntarily in response to an attractive early-retirement package was a forgotten element of the story. Instead, their departure became a defining moment in the institution's history, when trusting relationships between faculty and administrators gave way to suspicion and a divided community.

Most of the public colleges and universities in this study were unionized. Because union contracts circumscribe administrative discretion, these institutions have had less flexibility in cutting costs. The common strategy has been to freeze faculty lines and salaries and not to replace faculty who retire, die, or find employment elsewhere.

Unlike faculty at private colleges and universities, tenured faculty and most of the tenure-track faculty at public institutions felt relatively secure in their jobs. They were upset by the unpredictability of revenues. Sometimes their campus budgets were cut in midyear, after contracts had been signed. They were also disturbed by the grinding repetition of the reductions. Just as every cutback seemed to be the last that they would have to endure, another would appear on the horizon.

Becoming More Competitive

As Aldrich (1979) suggested, colleges and universities have reacted to increased competition and a decline in the college-age population by competing more vigorously. Private institutions, less fettered by governmental red tape, electoral politics, and collective bargaining agreements, have reacted most aggressively. They have intensified their recruiting efforts, developing glossy new brochures and hiring additional recruiters and professional enrollment management firms to conduct market research. Public colleges have undertaken similar efforts on a modest scale. Both public and private dependent colleges have eased admission standards in the hopes of attracting a larger pool of applicants.

Like corporations that believe they have saturated the market with a small number of products, dependent colleges and universities have diversified. They have introduced new programs and degrees that would be more attractive to students, especially older, nontraditional students, who represent an increasing proportion of college students (see Table 2–2). New England College (see Box 2–1) and Seattle University,

TABLE 2–2   Changes in the Portrait of "Traditional" College Students, 1970–1991

Student Category	1970 (percentage)	1991 (percentage)
All students		
Female[a]	41.2	55.2
Minority[b]	11.8[b]	21.2
Under 25 years old[a]	72.2	58.2
Over 34 years old[a]	9.6	17.9
Part-time	32.2	43.5
Undergraduates only		
Female[a]	42.3[c]	55.4
Minority[b]	—[b]	22.1
Under 25 years old	NA	64.2
Over 34 years old	NA	15.6
Part-time	28.4[c]	40.1

Adapted from *Lessons of a Generation: Education and Work in the Lives of the High School Class of 1972* by Clifford Adelman, 1994, San Francisco, Jossey-Bass Publishers, Table 6.4, p. 249, which was constructed from data in *Digest of Education Statistics, 1993* by T. D. Snyder, 1993, Washington, DC: National Center for Education Statistics, pp. 174, 177, 178, 180, 187, 188, and 206, and *The Condition of Education: 1981 Edition* by N. B. Dearman and V. W. Plisko, 1981, Washington, DC: National Center for Education Statistics, p. 142. Adapted with permission from Jossey-Bass Publishers.

[a]U.S. citizens only.

[b]Race/ethnicity data for 1970 are not comparable to those of later years. They cannot be estimated at all for the undergraduate population.

[c]Includes unclassified undergraduate students.

NA = not ascertained

for example, are among the many colleges and universities that have expanded offerings of professional programs, adding such majors as business, computer science, and human services. Some competitive strategies dramatically altered an institution's mission. For example, two women's colleges, Albertus Magnus and Colby-Sawyer, turned coeducational during the 1980s; and Green Mountain College, formerly a two-year college, became a four-year, baccalaureate-granting institution.

BOX 2–1　Close-up: New England College

New England College, a liberal arts institution with a campus in bucolic Henniker, New Hampshire, England, has New England charm. Although the college was founded in 1946, most of its buildings are old, built in another century, with slanting floors, stone fireplaces, and pastoral views from multipaned windows.

In addition to its liberal arts offerings, New England now provides programs in specifically career-directed fields, such as education, communications, and business. With a 1995/96 enrollment of approximately 700 students, it is heavily dependent upon tuition for operating revenues.

New England College began offering new professional degrees in the 1970s in the hopes of enticing more vocationally minded students to the campus. By the mid-1980s its faculty were deeply divided about the wisdom of this path. Some rejected attempts by the mostly liberal arts college curriculum committee to strengthen the general education curriculum. Soon after this, the New England Association of Schools and Colleges suggested that the college had strayed far from its liberal arts mission. It recommended that the college change its mission to reflect better the status quo.

The president of the college agreed with this assessment. However, many in the faculty opposed the recommendation. The president was replaced by another who, not coincidentally, had a reputation as an advocate of the liberal arts. He called for a renewal of the liberal arts at New England College.

Another team sent by the regional accrediting agency supported the college's decision to reemphasize its liberal education program. The college soon began a new general education reform effort.

(Continued)

BOX 2–1 *(Continued)*

From the outside, the curriculum that came out of the latest reform effort is impressive. Organized as a series of skills and perspective courses, it is multidisciplinary, international, multicultural, Western, and non-Western. Students take innovative core courses in natural science, the world community, and cultural diversity. Writing courses run across three years of the college's four-year curriculum. Inside, however, the faculty have grumbled. Some believe that the new curriculum was "pushed down their throats." Feeling compromised by the process, many faculty have wanted no part of the outcome of the reorganization.

In recent years the structure of the program has been modified to accommodate a smaller faculty. The delivery of the curriculum has undergone major revisions. Co-curricular activities, such as special symposia, have been linked with two core courses, in cultural diversity and human rights, now required for all first-year students. First-year seminars have common texts and are directly linked to writing courses taken during the same period. A proposed capstone course on world community is in the early stages of implementation.

Accelerating Responses to Market Changes

One change that has greatly upset faculty is their diminished role in decision making in their institutions. By almost all accounts, the culture of gradual change, consensual decision making, and faculty authority has given way to more centralized and rapid decision making. Administrators believe that the very survival of their institutions depends upon rapid and bold action. Sometimes, as in Albertus Magnus College's decision to become coeducational, faculty contributed to discussion of the issue but were largely left out of the decision making. Often faculty are prodded to the point where they feel they have no choice but to make reforms that the administrators believe are necessary.

Faculty view this change toward more centralized decision making as creating a deep schism in their community. What was once commonality of purpose and standards, especially in small colleges, has become a struggle pitting faculty against administrators. Mindful of their declining power, some faculty have withdrawn from active involvement in campus affairs. An administrator at one of the institutions in this study observed that the feeling of disconnection on his campus had been growing since the mid- to late 1970s. "Faculty," he said, "feel this particularly. They feel that they no longer have as much of a say and that there is too much management and not enough faculty initiative." But he did not blame faculty for this view. "They are right. The administration is too much a top-down affair." With the turmoil of the last two decades it is not surprising that faculty morale at many institutions is low.

SURVEY FINDINGS: THE CATALYSTS FOR GENERAL EDUCATION REFORM

For more than 30 years, public reports have criticized the quality of postsecondary education, especially in the liberal arts. A 1977 report of the Carnegie Foundation for the Advancement of Teaching claimed that "general education . . . is poorly defined and is so diluted with options that it has no recognizable substance of its own" (p. 184). By the 1980s the public outcry for general education reform had intensified. By the 1990s that outcry had turned into deep frustration with the seeming inability of colleges and universities to change general education significantly.

The failure to reform the general education curriculum was not because faculty were satisfied with the status quo. Both the telephone survey and campus visits revealed overwhelming faculty dissatisfaction with the loose distribution system that was in place before they undertook general education reform. In most cases the existing program, an outgrowth of curricular movements popular in the early 1970s, was seen to lack breadth and depth. In many cases it was criticized as well for having no clear philosophical basis. Faculty were concerned about student overspecialization in professional studies and the tendency to be overly career-minded. They were also dismayed by weaknesses in students' basic skills.

The telephone survey of administrators asked about the initiators of general education reform on their campuses. More than any other group, campus administrators were identified as being responsible for launching general education reform. The telephone survey indicated that administrators were the initiators of reform on 67 percent of the campuses (see Table 2–3). Faculty were identified as catalysts for general education reform on 32 percent of the campuses; accrediting agencies were identified as catalysts on 15 percent of the campuses. Other external factors, such as new regulations for general

TABLE 2–3   Initiators of General Education Reform

Initiator	n^a	$\%^a$
Administration	50	67
Faculty	24	32
Accrediting agency	11	15
Other external agent (e.g., state higher education agency, foundation)	7	9

Data are from telephone survey and campus visits.

[a]Frequencies add to more than 75 and percentages to more than 100 percent due to multiple responses.

education introduced by governing bodies, accounted for 9 percent.

Detailed interviews from the case-study institutions provide somewhat different accounts of the origins of general education reform. These interviewees, most of whom were faculty members, viewed stimuli external to the institution as more important than did administrators interviewed in the telephone survey. Interviewees in more than half the schools identified the pressure for changing the general education curriculum as arising from the actions and decisions of outside public agencies. In addition, fewer of those interviewed identified administrators as initiating reform efforts. This discrepancy between the findings of the telephone survey and those of the personal interviews might be due to the difficulty of pinpointing when a change process starts. It may also be significant that respondents in the telephone survey were academic administrators, whereas a majority of those interviewed on campuses were faculty. Members of each group had different perspectives on the role of administrators in general education reform.

It was difficult to identify exactly what propelled the general education change process on the campuses visited. Many of the colleges and universities in this study were in a great deal of turmoil just before the period of general education reform. Several conditions may have contributed to setting a campus on the road to curriculum reform. When did the process begin? Was it one event or a mixture of events that served as the catalyst? The varied responses mirrored the particular role of the persons being interviewed as well as the multitude of environmental stresses on each of the campuses.

For two institutions—the University of Maine at Machias and the University of Minnesota, Morris—state higher education agencies were the catalysts of record. In 1979, at the request of the University of Maine system, the president of Machias named a long-range planning committee, which recommended a review of the general education curriculum (see

Box 2–2). When the president of the University of Minnesota urged the campuses under his jurisdiction to become more differentiated from one another, he recommended that the Morris campus strengthen its liberal arts mission. The campus responded affirmatively and set up committees to improve its liberal arts curriculum.

For one institution—the University of Hartford in Connecticut—a change in state policy legitimated a general education reform that had already begun. In 1986 the Connec-

---

BOX 2–2   Close-up: University of Maine at Machias

The easternmost campus in the United States, the University of Maine at Machias lies in a remote northeast portion of coastal Maine, a two-hour trip from Bangor, the closest major city. Machias, entered over a roaring river gorge, is a small, simple village of mostly older storefronts, a few newer shops, and recently installed Victorian streetlamps. The rural campus, set on a small hill, has buildings of older, unadorned brick.

Established in 1909 as a normal school, the university developed in time into a state teachers college. In 1968, it joined the newly created University of Maine system as one of its seven campuses. At that time it widened both its mission and its offerings, becoming a multipurpose institution granting two- and four-year degrees; its curriculum emphasized education and business studies. During the 1970s the university further expanded to include such programs as environmental science and recreation management.

The university is a regional institution. Its mission, according to its president, "is to provide educational opportunities for citizens of Eastern Maine, in particular,

BOX 2–2 *(Continued)*

and Maine, in general." It supplies, for example, about 75 percent of the public school teachers for the region. With no community college in the area, the university provides opportunities for students to explore higher education through a de facto open admissions policy, allowing anyone to enroll in a course. Of just under 1,000 enrollees in 1991, 63 percent were in four-year baccalaureate programs, 20 percent were in two-year associate degree programs, and 17 percent were in nondegree programs. Women outnumbered men two to one. Traditional-age students (24 years and under) were 55 percent of the student population. There were 38 full-time faculty members, and class sizes ranged from 22 to 47 students. The student body was predominantly first-generation.

In 1979, at the request of the University of Maine system, the president of Machias named a Long Range Planning Committee to study the university's 10-year goals. Among its recommendations was one to review the general education curriculum. The College Curriculum Committee began to discuss the "Core" program, established in 1972 as a smorgasbord of offerings. At an open faculty meeting it was generally agreed that the core curriculum should be revised. Several needs for reorganization were perceived: the need to provide students with a shared experience in a more structured program; the need to create a strong liberal arts background for students entering professional fields; and the need for faculty "ownership," the sense of having a part in the formulation of the general education curriculum. The Core Curriculum Committee, a 10-member task force with representatives from each of the five divisions, four students, and the vice-president for academic affairs, was constituted in 1981. It obtained a consultancy grant from the National

(Continued)

BOX 2-2   *(Continued)*

Endowment for the Humanities to review the old Core, examined literature on general education, and explored materials from other campuses.

The committee established objectives for the new Core by revising the Student Needs Statement. The revised statement, accepted by the faculty in July 1982, called for (1) entry-level skills in reading, writing, and mathematics (with provision for testing and remediation); (2) competencies in oral and written communication, reading, quantitative thinking, and research; (3) methods of inquiry—historical, scientific, artistic, philosophical, and literacy; and (4) concepts that influence contemporary thought. The Core aims first at fulfilling objectives of the Student Needs Statement. A second goal is "to expose the students to an examination and scholarly study of issues and concerns of the modern society. . . ." Third, the Core encourages "the student to sample the wide variety of academic disciplines afforded by the University."

The new general education curriculum was instituted in the fall semester, 1983, without, according to one observer, "[spilling] a great deal of blood on the floor." Largely because the design process was an open one, with especially effective liaison between Core representatives and their divisions, the faculty evinced "a heightened awareness of the importance of a general education program."

Although not universally acclaimed, the Core, "a carefully crafted compromise," enjoys widespread support among the faculty and administration. Students feel the Core is effective in introducing them to an array of disciplines and is especially helpful to those seeking a major. A few changes were made in physical education requirements following a 1985 evaluation of the Core, but since then the basic curriculum has remained unchanged.

ticut higher education board mandated that one third of all courses at the baccalaureate level should be in the liberal arts. Administrators at the University of Hartford used this directive as leverage with the faculty to encourage change (see Box 2–3).

Regional accreditation agencies also acted as catalysts for reform. On three campuses in the study—New England College, Green Mountain College, and Plymouth State College—the results of an accreditation review included criticism of the general education curriculum. Anticipating criticism of their curricula, three other campuses—Colby-Sawyer College, Kean College (see Box 2–4), and Roger Williams College—made an effort to revise their general education curricula before scheduled accreditation reviews.

Interviewees on several campuses had conflicting perceptions about the origins of general education reform. For example, at Johnson State College several people attributed the general education initiative to the aftereffect of a mandate that schools in the Vermont higher educational system eliminate the duplication of programs. Under this mandate, Johnson State College could no longer offer majors in history and English. Suddenly faced with blanks in their schedules, faculty in these departments pressed for general education reform. They hoped to convince their colleagues to assign them to more general education courses. Not everyone interviewed, however, believed that the state system should be held accountable for what had happened. Some identified a single individual as the catalyst for change. Others believed that curricular reform was driven by administrators' desire to improve the college's reputation. According to one administrator, Johnson State College had acquired a reputation for taking any student. "We were getting a reputation as a dummy school." Some people attributed the change to declining enrollments, believing that faculty and administrators had embarked on general education reform as a way to increase the student body (see Box 2–5).

BOX 2–3   Close-up: University of Hartford

An independent, comprehensive university, the University of Hartford is located in West Hartford, an immediate suburb of Hartford, the capital of Connecticut. It was formed by the merger in 1957 of three independent colleges—the Hartford Art School, the Hartt School of Music, and Hillyer College, an arts and sciences institution—established between 1877 and 1920. Today the university, governed by a self-perpetuating board of trustees, in addition to its founding components comprises the College of Arts and Sciences; Barney School of Business and Public Administration; the College of Education, Nursing, and Health Professions; Engineering College; Ward College of Technology; and Hartford College for Women. These nine colleges collectively serve more than 5,200 full- and part-time undergraduates and about 1,800 graduate students.

   In the early 1980s three constituencies on campus converged to focus on general education. In 1983, the university received a three-year grant from the Andrew W. Mellon Foundation to develop a new general education curriculum for the College of Arts and Sciences. The Mellon grant gave faculty the opportunity to develop and teach a series of interdisciplinary courses. Encouraged by the results, the college faculty committee recommended a general education curriculum that would span the entire university, one that would "take advantage of the diversity and richness of our [schools and] colleges." Simultaneously, on the administrative level, the provost and council of deans began to argue for a common set of courses or educational experiences that would draw upon resources across the university. Lastly, the regents, wanting to ensure that students were being graduated with certain

BOX 2–3 *(Continued)*

core competencies and understandings, initiated discussions of a university-wide curriculum.

The Select Committee for a general education curriculum, appointed in 1985 by the provost, proposed in 1986 a 12-credit liberal education curriculum for all baccalaureate students. In the interim the state board for higher education mandated that one third of all undergraduate course work in Connecticut colleges and universities, public and private, be a "balanced distribution of required courses or restricted electives in the humanities, arts, natural and physical sciences, mathematics, and social sciences"—a regulation greeted as reinforcing the committee's own proposal. A university-wide curriculum committee was then appointed to review, develop, and implement the general education program.

Upon approval by the faculty senate, the university-wide general education curriculum became operational in fall 1987. Baccalaureate students were now required to select one course from each of four of five categories—Western Heritage, Other Cultures, the Arts, Social Context, and Science and Technology. Four or five courses are available in each category. All courses include traditional knowledge as well as the study of contemporary issues and problems "integrated in interdisciplinary courses that seek to synthesize ideas and make clear the relationships and connections among disciplines." The courses emphasize the development of "essential abilities and skills"—oral and written communication, analysis and problem solving, values analysis and independent decision making, social interaction, and civic responsibility.

The general education curriculum has drawn favorable comment in its initial years. Media attention has been positive. Faculty who have taught in the program have,

(Continued)

BOX 2–3   *(Continued)*

with some exceptions, been enthusiastic in their evaluations. The administration credits the curriculum with forg-
ing a new sense of unity. In subsequent years, although a
number of the all-curriculum courses have been revised,
changes in the general education curriculum have been
minimal. In 1992, the University of Hartford was one of
16 institutions selected by the Association of American
Colleges and Universities to be part of a working group of
institutions committed to strengthening and supporting
their general education curricula.

BOX 2–4   Close-up: Kean College of New Jersey

Founded in 1855 as a teacher-training institute, Kean
College of New Jersey has twice expanded the scope of its
mission. When its campus moved from Newark, New Jersey to Union in 1958, the college widened its major programs in the arts and sciences. In 1966, under the aegis of
the Higher Education Act, Kean became a multipurpose
educational institute. In the three decades since then the
college has developed strong programs not only in the liberal arts and sciences but also in professional areas such as
administrative sciences and health fields.

One of nine New Jersey state colleges, Kean presents
itself as "a major regional institution of higher learning
serving students from the communities of New Jersey and
its neighboring states." Its student body of 12,000 is increasingly diverse, as minority enrollment continues to
rise. In the decade between 1980 and 1989, African American matriculation grew from 11 percent to 14 percent,

BOX 2–4 *(Continued)*

while the Hispanic student population grew from 8 percent to 10.5 percent. In the same period the percentage of nonminority students dropped from 78 percent to 70 percent.

The demographics among full-time faculty continue to change similarly. During the 1980s, African American faculty increased from 3 percent to 7 percent, Hispanics from 3 percent to 5.5 percent, and Asian Americans from 2 percent to 4 percent. The number of women full-time faculty likewise rose, from 33 percent to 37 percent. The nonminority faculty declined from 91.5 percent to 83.5 percent.

During the 1980s, Kean underwent two academic reorganizations, from a two-school institution (Education, Arts and Sciences) to three schools and, ultimately, four (Education; Humanities, Social and Administrative Sciences; Natural Sciences, Nursing and Mathematics; and Business, Government and Technology).

Since the early 1970s the general education requirements have called for all students to take English composition as well as defined credit hours (CHs) in several academic "clusters," or breadth areas: humanities (12 CHs), social sciences and history (12 CHs), natural sciences and mathematics (7 CHs), and physical education and health (2–3 CHs). Impelled in 1980 by the state board of higher education's dictum that "approximately one-half of the student's time during a . . . baccalaureate program should be devoted to acquiring a solid base in understanding the . . . accumulated store of . . . [human] knowledge" and by an imminent accreditation visit, Kean took up the matter of its general education program. A Resolution Committee presented a final proposal in March 1984, calling for students to complete six three-credit core courses.

(Continued)

BOX 2–4   *(Continued)*

The core courses include: Composition (introduction to expository writing); Emergence of the Modern World (origins of 20th-century political, economic, and social systems); Intellectual and Cultural Traditions of Western Civilization, 1450 to the Present (introduction to philosophic attitudes and artistic sensibilities of Western peoples); Inquiry and Research (analysis of published research, conducting a research project); Landmarks of World Literature (representative readings); and Science and Technology in the Modern World (interrelatedness of science, technology, and society). A distinctive feature of this new program is the requirement that students attend two "cultural events" per core course.

College-wide implementation of the general education plan began in 1985/86. Implementing the new breadth-course requirements, which guide students toward further studies in the liberal disciplines, was delayed until fall 1991. Under these requirements, students must take introductory and intermediate-level courses in a minimum of nine disciplines divided into five broad categories: humanities, social and behavioral sciences, biological and physical sciences, mathematical sciences, and health and physical education.

Since 1992 no major changes have been made. In 1993, the program was reviewed internally and also evaluated by an outside consultant. Recently the faculty senate passed a series of recommendations on the general education program and specifically on linkages within the program and between the program and the majors; sequential development of skills; diversity; increased emphasis on science, mathematics, and technology; and increased emphasis on values. Program changes based upon these recommendations are expected to be made over the next five years.

BOX 2–5   Close-up: Johnson State College

Johnson State College, in Johnson, Vermont, nestles on a hillside against a backdrop of rolling hills and rounded mountains. The black iron fences and brick walls that separate so many New England colleges from their towns are here replaced by fields and stands of pines. Located in the northwest corner of the state, 36 miles north of Burlington, it is one of three state colleges, with a mission that stresses expanding access to liberal and professional education; supplying educated workers for the Vermont economy; and maintaining the quality of cultural, social, and economic life for all of Vermont. In 1991, the student population topped 1,400 undergraduates; 55 faculty held rank, well over half at the assistant professor level.

For a variety of reasons, by the 1980s many campus constituents were certain that new educational policies, including a general education curriculum, were needed. An ad hoc committee named by the president was charged with developing a new undergraduate curriculum. The committee met twice a week over the summer and presented its proposals to the faculty in the fall. The plan called for a "three-school system"—two years of general education followed by either two years of professional study or two years of liberal arts.

With no direct participation during the design sessions, the faculty quickly rebelled at the proposal, which was deemed "dead on arrival." As one observer indicated: "We were taking away from departmental offerings. . . . When you make even a slight change in a small school, it has a big impact on departmental programs. The faculty resisted because they feared enrollment losses in their departments and in their courses."

(Continued)

BOX 2–5   *(Continued)*

A second attempt was made, and a more open, inclusive approach was adopted. Both the president and the college's curriculum committee held a series of informal meetings, often over dinner, to bring more faculty into the process. About 75 percent of the faculty added their voices to the debate, and observers reported an air of collaboration and trust. One observer noted that both the academic and the vocational faculties "did a lot of horse trading because everyone knew that they needed a piece of the [general education program] pie."

A new ad hoc committee was formed, specifically charged with redesigning the general education component of the overall curriculum. It soon became apparent that both the general education committee and the faculty assembly agreed that mathematics, English, and a variety of disciplinary courses should be required. They disagreed, however, on how the disciplinary courses should be distributed (i.e., how many credits would be assigned to each division), how significant a part some newly developed interdisciplinary courses should play, how many total credits the general education program should include, and how much student choice should be allowed. According to one source, general education was seen by some as

> taking away from the major. . . . Some majors required up to 75 credit hours, such as physical therapy and hotel management. . . . What's odd [about Johnson State] is that the "training" faculty are uppity. They don't feel looked down upon. This is disconcerting to the academic faculty, especially since the new curriculum had to be toned down to get a pabulum acceptable to all. It was considered a big victory to get a maximum of 60 hours for a major. That's one half [the credits needed] for graduation! So we [later] got a weak general education program.

BOX 2–5   *(Continued)*

After a full year of deliberation the process stalled. Whether it was due to loss of interest or the feeling that too many compromises had been made or that the interdisciplinary component was too ambitious is difficult to say. However, events overtook the faculty. To reduce what it saw as duplication within the system, the state college board of trustees eliminated the English and history majors at Johnson State. Now believing that their positions were even more in jeopardy and that the student interest would be better served as well, the faculty assembly in 1983 approved a new general education curriculum. Administrative approval followed within the week.

A decade later, in 1993, the college undertook a five-year planning program to reform its general education curriculum. Proposals are being pilot-tested, after which the most successful are expected to be integrated into a new general education curriculum.

On four campuses—Bridgewater State College, Plymouth State College, Seattle University, and the University of Hartford—faculty and administrators described their campuses as having been relatively stable at the time of general education reform. Turmoil was clearly in the past. Seattle University, one of the two private institutions in this group, had weathered declining enrollments and near bankruptcy in the late 1960s and early 1970s. Bridgewater State College in Massachusetts and Plymouth State College in New Hampshire were public institutions where the draconian budget cuts of the early 1990s had not yet hit. Enrollments were healthy. Faculty were unionized. They respected their chief academic officers. On all four campuses insiders were identified as the initial catalysts for reform.

CONNECTING PAST TO PRESENT

In organizational studies of higher education, colleges and universities are frequently described as "loosely coupled organizations." Coined by Karl Weick (1976), this phrase refers to a system of elements in an organization that are weakly connected to one another. Although the elements may be responsive to one another, they are independent entities with their own cultures and communities. Especially appealing to students of higher education, this theoretical construct makes sense of what at first glance appear to be highly anarchic and decentralized organizations. It offers an explanation of why changing colleges and universities is such a difficult task.

What happens when external stimuli are so powerful that all units are affected? The evidence on the campuses in this study suggests that environmental turmoil tightens the loosely coupled relationships among elements in the system. Most of the colleges and universities visited had weathered crises precipitated by one or more of the three changing conditions in the environment (resources, market, and external influences and control). As critical events piled up, they occasioned changes in the way these institutions operated. Decision making was centralized. Costs were cut. Programmatic changes were made rapidly, with limited faculty input. The cumulative effect of externally induced crises and internal responses to crises was strongly felt, especially by the faculty. New attitudes replaced old beliefs about campus culture, work routines, and community. Economic insecurity made faculty and administrators wary of their colleagues and anxious about their futures.

▶ 3

Inside the
Change Process

Reforming the curriculum is always
difficult and fraught with perils.
—*JERRY GAFF (1983, p. 164)*

A PERILOUS JOURNEY

As colleges and universities cope with the increasingly turbulent atmosphere of higher education and the internal schisms that seem to intensify in this environment, it is remarkable that so many have undertaken to reform general education. Successful curricular change requires careful maneuvering among the myriad internal and external interests of an institution of higher education. A careful mapping of the change process, then, from consultation to proposal to implementation, is instructive. This chapter looks at the process close up. Drawing on data from the telephone survey of 71 institutions and 15 campus visits, the chapter looks at the underpinnings of organizational change, reviews the survey findings concerning the design and implementation of a new curriculum, and illustrates the design process through a discussion of events on several campuses.

Design of General Education

The Committee

General education reform on college campuses is usually marked by the appointment of a committee responsible for recommending a new program. Table 3–1 summarizes telephone survey data on the characteristics of design committees. Not surprisingly, the committees varied greatly in their size, composition, and duration of work. Slightly more than half (54 percent) of the campuses appointed an ad hoc committee to undertake the redesign of general education, whereas the remainder (46 percent) charged the standing curriculum committee, or one of its subcommittees, with the task. Administrators were solely responsible for making appointments to the design committees on two thirds of the campuses, whereas faculty participated in such appointments on one third of the campuses.

Faculty members generally chaired the design committees, although administrators (a provost, dean, or academic vice-president) did so on about one third of the campuses.

Committee sizes ranged from 3 to 35 members, with an average of 11 members. The committee composition reflected different configurations of faculty, administrators, and department or division chairpersons. The most popular committee configuration included both administrators and at-large faculty members, followed by committees composed of only at-large faculty. Relatively few department and division chairpersons participated in design committees. The committees tended to have a predominance of liberal arts faculty, with professional and technical faculty in the minority.

Duration

A relatively short but labor-intensive period was typical for designing a new general education curriculum. About half of the campuses reported that their design groups met once a

TABLE 3–1   Characteristics of General Education Design Committees

Characteristic		%[a]
Committee Type		
Ad hoc committee		54
Standing curriculum committee		46
Appointments to Ad Hoc Committees Made by		
Administrators		67
Faculty		18
Both administrators and faculty		15
Chairperson of Design Committee		
Faculty member		63
Provost, dean, or vice-president of academic affairs		37
Size of Design Committee		
3–6 members		19
7–10 members		40
11–14 members		17
15+ members		23
Design Committee Composition (Position)		
Administrators and at-large faculty		52
At-large faculty only		27
Administrators, department chairs, and at-large faculty	14	
Administrators and department chairs		4
Department chairs and at-large faculty		4
Design Committee Composition (Area)		
Only liberal arts faculty		30
Mostly liberal arts faculty		60
Only professional/technical faculty		5
Mostly professional/technical faculty		5

Data are from telephone survey.

[a]Percentages may not add to 100 percent due to rounding.

week or more, with the remainder meeting on a biweekly or monthly basis. Among those who were able to make an estimate (and most could not) of the total hours of meeting time, the median was 39 hours, with a range from 12 to 420 hours (see Table 3–2). For the total span of time; most campuses studied general education over a period of 9 months to 2 years; the median duration was 1 year. The median time from the

TABLE 3–2   Duration of Design Process

Duration Measure	*n*	Median	Minimum	Maximum
Total design hours	30	39	12	420
Total number of design months	48	12	1	84
Years from beginning of design discussion until implementation	50	2.5	< 1	12

Data are from telephone survey.

initiation of discussions about design to the actual implementation of a revised general education program was 2.5 years. The range was substantial: A few campuses (4 percent) accomplished the feat in the same year; most campuses (60 percent) took between 1 and 3 years to design and implement a new program; and 36 percent took 4 or more years to do so. One campus implemented its program 12 years after discussions began.

No clear relationship exists between the length of time that the design group met and the amount of change in the new general education curriculum compared with the preexisting curriculum. For 18 campuses that experienced minor changes in their general education curricula the median number of months that the design group met was 12 (see Table 3–3). For 13 campuses with moderate change to their programs the median was 13 months. Eight campuses in the study experienced a great amount of change with a median of only 11 months to design it.

A Closer Look at Actual Campuses

These summary numbers indicate the wide range of committee profiles that produce a new general education curriculum.

TABLE 3–3   Duration of Design Process, Shown by Extent of Curriculum Change

Amount of Change	n	Median Number of Months	Minimum Number of Months	Maximum Number of Months
Minimum	18	12	2	48
Moderate	13	13	1	84
Great	8	11	2	24

Data are from telephone survey

Committees may be preexisting or ad hoc, small or large; they may meet for a short period or a lengthy one. Understanding the substantive work of the design committees, however, requires a closer look at the context in which they work. Bridgewater State College in Massachusetts and Green Mountain College in Vermont provide two very different contexts for understanding the design process in general education reform. The Bridgewater campus experienced a curriculum development process that was universally viewed as open and inclusive. At Green Mountain the general education program was designed behind closed doors.

On the Bridgewater campus the curriculum committee charged an ad hoc subcommittee with changing the general education program (see Box 3–1). Members representing a range of disciplines volunteered for this task. No single group dominated the committee, which was chaired by a well-respected senior faculty member.

In its first year the Bridgewater subcommittee on general education was divided into three task forces. The first was charged with gathering information about current students. Members collected data concerning choice of majors, Scholastic Aptitude Test (SAT) scores, and course-taking patterns. The second task force analyzed the results of alumni surveys conducted annually by the college's career planning

BOX 3–1   Close-up: Bridgewater State College

Bridgewater State College in Bridgewater, Massachusetts is located about an hour's drive from Boston on a picturesque 129-acre campus. The approximately 270 full-time faculty are unionized. Most of its 8,200 students are from the southeastern region of the state, and many are first-generation college students. About half begin their studies directly after being graduated from high school, and most stay in the area after graduation. Because of its large population of nontraditional students and its curriculum, which merges liberal arts and professional education, the college administration sees Bridgewater as an educational service center for the region.

In November 1991 the campus—along with other Massachusetts state colleges and universities—was in the throes of a budget crisis, having suffered legislative funding cuts for several successive years. During this period the college enjoyed an energetic and talented administration which balanced the books with a minimum of sacrifice and a faculty with remarkably high morale. The college boasted a strong liberal arts program and excellent teacher education. The faculty believed that the college was better than any other in the state system.

The impetus for changing the general education curriculum came from the faculty. In the early 1980s the general education program was a loosely structured menu system in which almost any course could fulfill the requirement in its area of study. The program was perceived to have no guiding philosophy, coherence, or structure. During the 1983/84 academic year the curriculum committee formed a seven-member ad hoc subcommittee representing a range of disciplines and charged it with reforming the program. After a short term of leadership by one individual the helm was taken by a department

BOX 3–1 *(Continued)*

head who adopted the strategy of getting people to discuss their differences with one another. Dozens of hearings were scheduled to get feedback on the design of the evolving program.

In fall 1984 the subcommittee proposed the inclusion of 12 areas in the new general education program: writing, speaking, philosophy, locating and processing information, history, literature, artistic modes of expression, physical and biological sciences, behavioral and social sciences, foreign language, mathematics, and non-Western civilization. A key element of the proposal was a set of criteria designed to define the types of courses that would be approved under this program. Although two new elements were introduced into the general education curriculum—a foreign language requirement and a course in non-Western civilization—the new program was not a radical departure from the old. The new criteria for courses in the curriculum, however, made general education "a whole new ball game": All general education courses would have to be approved by the subcommittee.

After much discussion and minor revision of the proposal, the new general education program was approved. The fall of 1985 was spent preparing for its implementation. Extensive meetings with department chairs were held to prepare course proposals and develop a book to describe the new program.

Like the design process, the review of courses for the general education curriculum was open. The agendas of subcommittee meetings were published, and department chairs were informed when their offerings were to be discussed. Votes were made in public, and copies of minutes were sent to department chairs. Subcommittee decisions could be appealed to the curriculum committee.

(Continued)

BOX 3-1   *(Continued)*

The implementation of the new program, however, proved somewhat bumpy. Resources had to be reallocated to the foreign languages department to staff introductory courses, and faculty found that no incentives existed to develop courses in non-Western civilization. With no central office or officer charged with directing implementation of the program, students were confused about which rules applied to them, and faculty were seldom prepared to advise them well. Class-size limits were too high, especially in writing-intensive courses. Students complained that the high number of credits consumed by the general education program significantly limited their ability to enroll in electives.

Notwithstanding these difficulties the faculty were largely satisfied with the outcome of the program redesign, due in large part to the integrity of the subcommittee and the process employed. The design and implementation were almost universally viewed as fair; an unusually large number of faculty took part in an atmosphere of commitment. Although there is discussion on campus about initiating a review of the program, no changes have been made since the redesign.

office. The third reviewed general education requirements at selected colleges in New England. In addition, the subcommittee sent questionnaires to five groups: alumni classes from 1945 to 1975, alumni classes from 1976 to 1982, regional employers, current juniors and seniors, and faculty. Finally, the subcommittee scheduled 27 hearings, often three times a week, with individual departments to solicit opinions about the goals of a new general education program.

In the second year the subcommittee developed a guiding philosophy for general education, identified 12 areas of study to be included in the program, and devised criteria to define the types of courses that would be approved under this program. The proposal was delivered to the curriculum committee, which held hearings. Discussion, debate, and some tinkering ensued, and the proposal was approved pretty much intact. It was then forwarded to the all-college committee and to the president for approval. (A unionized campus, Bridgewater does not have a faculty senate or faculty meetings per se.)

Besides having fair-minded leadership and an open process, Bridgewater exemplifies the use of research, an effort advocated by Daniel Seymour (1988), who argued that data should be collected and examined during all stages of an academic change process. Although Bridgewater used data and consulted with the campus at every juncture, the process was not without angst. Philosophical differences and personality problems cropped up, as might be expected in such an intensive and value-laden endeavor. The important point is that all parties perceived not only that they were consulted but also that they were heard.

Green Mountain College offers an example of a process that began as neither open nor inclusive (see Box 3–2). An administrator selected a group of chairpersons from the liberal arts to design a new general education curriculum. The committee was instructed to work in secret, in the belief that it would be better to avoid the opposition anticipated over such topics as reducing the number of credit hours in professional programs, giving up "pet courses," and developing new courses in all likelihood without release time. Additionally, the administrator believed that a stronger program could be developed if the committee was not second-guessed along the way. As information leaked from the committee and spread throughout campus, it inevitably became distorted. The faculty became both fearful and angry—exactly the situation that the administrator had hoped to avoid.

BOX 3–2   Close-up: Green Mountain College

Lying in a valley in the town of Poultney, Vermont—population 3,220—Green Mountain College is a movie-set New England college. Most of its buildings are brick colonial, some with columns and porticoes, and none more than four stories high. Walkways crisscross the main quadrangle, and stately maples reach into the sky.

Founded in 1834 as the Troy Conference Academy, in 1863 it became Ripley Female College, the first institution of higher learning in Vermont to grant a woman a baccalaureate degree. Eleven years later it reverted to its original name and became coeducational. In 1943, with a wartime shortage of male students, the college became a two-year college for women, renamed Green Mountain College. In 1974, it returned to coeducational, baccalaureate status. The college emphasized career programs until the late 1980s, when it expanded its liberal arts offerings and, through a new general education curriculum, began requiring students to combine liberal and career studies.

With an enrollment of 550, Green Mountain prides itself on providing small undergraduate classes and individual attention to students. Full-time faculty number 35; they are neither tenured nor unionized. Seven academic departments (education, fine arts, language and literature, science, management, recreation and leisure studies, and social sciences) offer a variety of programs. Though small and rural, Green Mountain is not a local college; most students are from out of state, with a handful from other countries. Most students are of traditional age.

The previous general education program was a menu system that required students to choose nine credit hours from each of three areas: science/math, humanities, and social sciences. Several forces contributed to a reform of

BOX 3–2　*(Continued)*

this loose distribution system. First among these forces was an accreditation visit by the New England Association of Schools and Colleges (NEASC) in 1982. NEASC was critical of the college's general education program and mandated an interim five-year review.

Second, a senior administrator took a keen interest in general education at Green Mountain. Believing that faculty were not opposed to revisions, he appointed a committee to design a new program. Traditionally at Green Mountain the academic dean appoints half of a committee's members and faculty elect the other half. In this case, however, the administrator selected the entire committee and named himself as chair.

Besides the distrust of nonparticipating faculty, the design committee faced an additional hurdle. The committee worked with the understanding that resources would be made available to support a new general education program. Operating under this assumption, it designed a sophisticated, detailed curriculum of core courses, multidisciplinary courses, and senior seminars. The trustees rejected the program because of the high cost of implementing it. The faculty—already predisposed to dislike it—argued that students were academically unprepared for the curriculum and that faculty would need release time to develop it, which the trustees were unwilling to support.

After this proposal was rejected, the general education committee began work on a second, more modest design. Faculty opinions and advice were sought through a survey, informal discussions, and presentations at faculty meetings. The campus was kept informed through the circulation of committee meeting minutes. The committee developed a mission statement and designed a 39-credit modified distribution system: backgrounds of human cul-

(Continued)

BOX 3–2   *(Continued)*

ture (6 credits), language and expression (6 credits), the scientific endeavor (12 credits), individual and social worlds (12 credits), and health and well-being (3 credits). Trustees and the faculty senate approved the design, with minor modifications, in 1988.

Spurred by a grant from the National Endowment for the Humanities in 1991 and criticisms from NEASC in 1992 concerning the size and lack of coherence of the cafeteria system, faculty discussions continued. In 1993, a broadly representative faculty committee was charged with assessing the general education program. The committee surveyed faculty, obtained information from other institutions, and held its deliberations in an open manner. A task force established in 1994 used the committee's recommendations to propose sweeping changes to the general education curriculum, emphasizing faculty "ownership." These changes were approved by the president and then discussed in special faculty meetings. In 1995, faculty overwhelmingly endorsed the task force recommendations for fall 1996. The new program, "Perspectives on the Environment," includes three core courses designed and taught by faculty from every discipline. It also includes an interwoven series of distribution courses linked to the core theme of the environment. A faculty governance council is responsible for implementation, assessment, and faculty development.

Other problems befell the design process at Green Mountain. Committee members perceived that they had support from the trustees to develop an ambitious new program. The committee thought that funds would be available to them, within reason, for the new general education program—for faculty to teach in the program and for other types of program support. A sophisticated curriculum was developed that included core courses, multidisciplinary courses, and senior seminars. The trustees, however, rejected the proposal based on the cost and subsequently issued a mandate that any new program must not entail new costs. The faculty, predisposed to dislike any proposal that came from a handpicked and cloistered committee, rejected it as well.

After the failure of the first proposal the committee regrouped and began work on a second program. Although the composition of the committee remained the same, its procedures did not. The committee now actively sought faculty feedback through informal discussions, a survey, presentations at general faculty meetings, and dialogue with the faculty senate.

The final proposal, much less ambitious than the first, offered a modified distribution system with more coherence than the existing system. After minor alterations the committee's proposal was approved by the trustees, faculty senate, and faculty at large.

The Green Mountain process was problematic from two important angles. First was the process itself: The closed, secretive approach engendered anxiety and anger among the very people who must deliver the final product to the students. As Seymour (1988) noted in discussing cultural impediments to innovation, individuals will resist an innovation unless they have been involved in its formulation.

Second, the committee was unrealistic about the resources that would be made available to support the new curriculum. Inattention to implementation issues during the design process undermines the entire effort when a large discrepancy exists between the resources needed for a new program and those available.

The work of design committees can be facilitated when consensus exists not only about available resources but also about the mission of the program. Gaff (1983) noted that early agreement by the faculty on a rationale and on basic elements makes it easier to design a curriculum: "In the absence of working agreements about the aims, content, or structure of general education, an institution simply cannot build a curriculum" (p. 164). Green Mountain learned this lesson the hard way. Other campuses avoided this error by acquiring early formal approval of general education concepts from their faculties. This method was employed at the University of Hartford and the University of Bridgeport in Connecticut, and Plymouth State in Plymouth, New Hampshire (see Box 3–3).

BOX 3–3   Close-up: Plymouth State College

Located in the small town of Plymouth in rural New Hampshire, Plymouth State College was established during the 19th century as a teachers college. In the early 1960s it expanded its programs, granting baccalaureate degrees in liberal arts and business as well as in teaching. Its student body, drawn from the surrounding region, numbers about 3,500, predominantly traditional-age students 18–22 years old. The college enjoys a healthy enrollment largely because of its popular professional programs in business and physical education. With a full-time faculty of approximately 140, the school is divided into 13 academic departments: art; business; computer science; education; English; foreign languages; health, physical education, and recreation; mathematics; music and theatre; natural science; philosophy; psychology; and social science.

From 1968 to the mid-1980s, general education changed little at Plymouth State. Students were required to take 12 credit hours in the humanities, 12 in social sciences, and 15 in sciences and mathematics and could be graduated without ever having taken a course in history or philosophy. The faculty, dissatisfied with the program, argued that it lacked breadth and depth. Further, they were cognizant of the growing national concern about

BOX 3–3   *(Continued)*

overspecialization and narrow career-mindedness in undergraduate programs.

In November 1983 the dean named an ad hoc committee to study the general education program and recommend changes. By the summer of 1984 the committee of senior faculty and the associate dean agreed on some minimum requirements: the need for communication and social, scientific, philosophical, historical, and aesthetic understandings as well as the need for some kind of integrative experience among the various disciplines.

From November 1984 through May 1985 the committee surveyed the faculty to ascertain their thinking on needed changes. The ad hoc group schooled itself in the literature on the subject and communicated with colleagues at other institutions concerning successful programs. Throughout its deliberations the committee kept the faculty informed of its work by using liaison members to meet regularly with the academic departments, sponsoring guest speakers and workshops, publishing a newsletter, and anticipating criticism and meeting it openly through handouts explaining its thinking and actions.

Despite some dissension, no opposition arose to reform in the general education program. The final proposal, submitted to the full faculty in May 1985, was accepted with no revisions. The faculty were pleased with the committee's work and felt that the process had been open and aboveboard and that ample opportunities for discussion had been provided.

The new proposal offered a conceptual framework for the general education program with five components: skills, perspectives (areas of knowledge or understanding), integrative or interdisciplinary courses, an emphasis on writing, and a requirement for the study of upper-level courses outside one's major. The proposal sought to

(Continued)

BOX 3–3   *(Continued)*

balance disciplinary content and methodology and stressed the skills of writing, speaking, and listening.

Since the proposal was implemented, no changes have been made, although minor improvements will likely be made over the next few years, particularly to give students more flexibility in choosing general education courses required by various majors.

Further Resources

In preparing to reform general education, committees at several campuses reviewed current literature, examined general education requirements at other campuses, or did both. For example, Bridgewater investigated requirements at other New England campuses; Plymouth State reviewed literature and contacted other campuses; and Green Mountain, even in its early "closed" attempt, sought information by reviewing the general education literature and visiting three nearby campuses.

Institutions sometimes retained outside consultants to assist in reviewing and redefining the general education curriculum. Some campuses received external grants to assist in the development of general education programs. A few campuses obtained these funds at the beginning of the design process (the University of Hartford and Seattle University), while others obtained funds in the implementation stage to aid in course design and faculty development (the University of Bridgeport, Albertus Magnus, and Kean College).

All campuses made diligent, well-considered efforts to improve general education. The typical design committee, an ad hoc one with 7–10 members appointed by an administrator, was composed of administrators and at-large faculty, predominantly from the liberal arts, with a faculty member as chair. Committees met once a week over a period of 12 months. Implementation occurred a year and a half after design completion. The more successful design committees were composed of a cross section of the various constituencies on campus, and these committees proceeded inclusively—seeking information and feedback from a wide range of sources.

"Closed" and, hence, unsuccessful design efforts were also good-faith attempts. These typically involved a visionary individual or a group of like-minded persons with shared notions about general education. Their desire was to offer a fully developed proposal of an innovative program that would make their campus unique in its bold approach to general education. Given the loosely coupled, decentralized nature of colleges and universities, however, consensus was too remote a possibility without the participation of each element.

CHALLENGES OF IMPLEMENTATION

Redesigning general education was an arduous task for the campuses. The debate over what constitutes an educated person was protracted and intense, with all participants having a deeply felt interest in the outcome. Consensus on educational philosophy and resource allocation could not be achieved quickly or easily, even on the most collegial of campuses.

Once the conceptual framework of general education was in place, committee members faced the task of translating plans into a realistic program—more meetings, discussion, disagreement, brokering, compromise. A new general education program was eventually produced and moved through appropriate channels for approval and, once passed, was ready to be carried out.

On most campuses, however, design committees failed to anticipate fully the implementation issues—particularly those related to responsibility and resources—that are crucial to the success of a general education program.

Responsibility

"The essential problem with the administration of general education is that, at most institutions, no one has the responsibility and authority to act on behalf of the program as a whole" (Gaff, 1983, p. 135). Data from the telephone survey corroborate Gaff's statement. On two thirds of campuses a committee (a standing curriculum committee or a general education committee) was charged with oversight of general education. Campus visits identified how this type of management tends to be carried out. The committee would retain formal oversight of the program, whereas departments would handle the so-called everyday responsibilities of staffing courses and, sometimes, monitoring course content. Bridgewater State managed its program this way. A subcommittee of the curriculum committee approved courses to be included in the general education program (save for two English courses); day-to-day management was handled at the department level. Only 9 percent of campuses employed a program director for general education, and 11 percent of campuses subsumed the responsibilities for the general education program under the duties of an academic officer (see Table 3–4).

TABLE 3–4   Oversight of General Education Program

Source of Oversight	*n*	%
Standing curriculum committee	27	47
General education committee	11	19
Provost, dean, or vice-president of academic affairs	6	11
Program director	5	9
Other	5	9
No oversight provided	3	5

Data are from telephone survey.

The management of general education was sometimes divided in rather creative ways. For example, at several institutions a director or a coordinator of general education oversaw interdisciplinary aspects of a program, while departments managed the discipline-based requirements. At Albertus Magnus, for example, a director coordinated level I (freshman) courses and level IV (capstone) courses, and departments were responsible for levels II and III.

Discrepancies existed, however, between the responsibility for general education and the authority for it. There was a difference between having responsibility for the day-to-day management of a general education program and having the authority to make decisions about the program. General education directors tended to have great responsibility and little authority, whereas curriculum and general education committees tended to have much authority but little responsibility, which was typically delegated to departments.

"Management by committee" was problematic on several counts. First, when day-to-day responsibilities were relegated to departments, important matters often went unresolved, such as advising students about general education. Second, when departments were responsible for their general education courses, these courses could, over time, come to reflect the interests of those in the department, as opposed to those who governed the general education program; in this way the overall program risked losing its distinctiveness. At Roger Williams College, for example, a new general education program was first created as an entity separate from the disciplinary divisions, with its own director (see Box 3–4). A campus reorganization elevated the divisions to schools, with a dean heading each. Responsibility for staffing and funding general education then moved to the individual schools and their deans, and courses were renamed to reflect the department instead of being called "General Education XXX." Because general education could no longer be identified as a separate division with its own courses, many on campus feared that the program would lose its flavor and sense of coherence. The worry was

BOX 3–4   Close-up: Roger Williams College

Roger Williams College in Bristol, Rhode Island is an independent coeducational institution offering liberal arts and selected professional degrees, including business, engineering, and architecture. Students may major in any of 31 fields of study.

The campus, beautifully sited overlooking Mount Hope Bay, is well groomed and relatively new, having been built in 1969. Most of the college's 2,000 full-time students live on campus and come from New England and mid-Atlantic states. Roger Williams employs 300 full- and part-time instructors. Average class size is 20 students.

The institution grew out of a branch campus of Northeastern University's School of Commerce, which was founded in 1919. When the college opened its Bristol campus in 1969, the curriculum reflected the times: The byword was relevance, and students had much freedom of choice. By the mid-1970s the faculty imposed some order by implementing a distribution system in which students were required to take at least one course from each of the divisions at the college. Faculty concern about the curriculum became further evident in 1981/82, when the College Curriculum Committee (CCC) discussed its dissatisfaction with the distribution requirements. Almost all faculty were concerned that students needed better preparation in composition and computation. For some faculty another problem was the lack of breadth in the students' college experience. The liberal distribution requirements meant that students could fulfill requirements without venturing far from their chosen field of study. In addition, some faculty thought that several of the majors required too many courses, thus limiting the students' opportunities for exploring other fields.

BOX 3–4 *(Continued)*

In preparing for a visit of the New England Association of Schools and Colleges (NEASC), the college initiated a curriculum review. The report of this self-study, based on the work of the CCC, concluded that the curriculum had "no perceived center or academic focus for either students or faculty." During academic years 1983/84 and 1985/86 the CCC documented the problems of the curriculum and designed a proposal that became the basis of the final version of the general education program. It included foundation or "skills" courses and required students to complete 10 courses (later 9) in seven disciplinary categories. An Ad Hoc Committee on General Education appointed to refine the program disagreed on the program's scope; number of courses; and competing emphases on intellectual processes, such as creative thinking, synthesis, and analysis versus specific course content. Business and technical faculty charged that the emphasis on humanities courses was a thinly veiled attempt of liberal arts faculty to protect their jobs by ensuring enrollment. In November 1985, despite sometimes vociferous opposition from an estimated 20–30 percent of the faculty, the proposal was passed.

Implementation was difficult. The first issue was how to reconcile the new program with the divisional structure of the institution. This was never resolved. A General Education Core Committee was created, and a half-time coordinator of general education was hired. Proposals for courses were solicited from the faculty, and assessment and evaluation mechanisms were devised. No one was sure what the budget should be, but the administration became increasingly concerned about program expenses, particularly those for part-time faculty and for assessment.

(Continued)

BOX 3–4   *(Continued)*

In 1990, a reorganization of the college called for divisions to become schools, each headed by a dean. With this reorganization, staffing and funding became the responsibility of school deans and not of a program coordinator. The program no longer existed as a separate entity.

A 1994 internal review of the general education curriculum led to major changes in the program. Since then students must take interdisciplinary core courses in five areas, including the sciences, Western civilization, social sciences, literature and philosophy, and the fine arts. They must also take a five-course core concentration in an academic area other than the major and, at the end of the college experience, an integrative senior seminar.

Despite implementation problems and the sometimes deep divides among faculty in the wake of the design and implementation processes, general education at Roger Williams is considered a success. One faculty member observed: "General education gives students a less myopic view of learning; they see learning as exploration, not memorization." Many faculty felt that the college benefited greatly from looking at the curriculum as a unified whole, rather than division by division, for the first time in the institution's history.

---

that these "general" courses would soon become so heavily identified with the divisions that no distinction would exist between discipline-based courses and general education courses. In effect, it was the first step back to the old, loose distribution system.

At the other end of the spectrum, "management by director" was not without its problems. Some directors of general education were frustrated by their lack of authority; awkward reporting relationships (often to a committee); and lack of status in the community, as they were members neither of the faculty nor of the administration.

Nevertheless, on campuses where a director was in place, better management of general education prevailed. Directors were able to monitor the quality and staffing of courses; oversee advising; ensure that courses were available to allow students to graduate on time (which requires sensitivity to the size of cohorts moving through the curriculum); offer support to faculty in the development of courses; and, in general, keep the spirit of the program alive. Problems were evident, however, when directors had few resources at their disposal. Without adequate resources, directors were unable, for example, to offer release time and development opportunities for faculty, elements critical to the success of any curricular innovation.

Resources

Resources were crucial to the successful implementation of the new general education program and, not surprisingly, difficult to obtain. About one third of the telephone survey respondents reported that budget constraints had made the implementation of general education difficult. Of the campuses visited, none said that there were adequate resources to support the general education program, particularly for faculty to prepare themselves for designing and teaching interdisciplinary courses.

Among campuses able to find funds for general education, about half patched together funding from a combination of sources (see Table 3–5). About one fourth of the campuses shifted some funds from the operating budget to cover the needs of the new general education program. Only 6 percent located special institutional funds or grant monies. The remaining 13 percent reallocated existing funds. Almost all campuses saw an erosion in the limited funding made available when their general education program was first implemented.

TABLE 3–5 Sources of Funds for Implementing New General Education Programs

Source of Funds	n^a	%
Combination of sources	25	53
Operating budget	13	28
Reallocation of existing funds	6	13
Special institutional funds	2	4
Outside grants	1	2

Data are from telephone survey.

[a]Base number represents campuses (47) that allocated resources for implementing new general education programs.

The telephone survey probed for specific areas where resources were expended (see Table 3–6). Two thirds (66 percent) of the campuses reported that they allocated resources to modifying orientation to prepare students for the new general education program, and 57 percent stated that they modified the advising program. Nevertheless, registrars interviewed on campus visits almost universally reported that the advising system regarding general education was poor, with considerable confusion concerning which students were to be "grandfathered" under the old general education guidelines, which were to be bound to the new ones, and what was to be done about transfer students. In addition, staff shortages often resulted in students' being closed out of general education courses. Horror stories were recounted of seniors who were unable to graduate for this reason. The implementation nightmares visited upon campus registrars might have been avoided—or at least mitigated—by ample planning during the design stage of the process.

Slightly more than half of the campuses reported allocating resources for the retraining of faculty members in teaching methods or subject area (see Table 3–6). This retraining was especially important because interdisciplinary courses

TABLE 3–6   Types of Expenditures for Implementing New General Education Programs

Type of Expenditure	n[a]	$\%$[b]
Modifications to student orientation	31	66
Faculty incentives for creating new courses 31	66	
New instructional materials	30	64
Revision of campus publications	29	62
Modifications to the advising program	27	57
Library upgrade	26	55
Retraining of faculty in teaching methods or subject	26	55
Hiring of new faculty	25	53
Revision of campus mission statement	8	17
Revision of admissions policies or procedures	8	17

Data are from telephone survey.

[a]Base number represents campuses (47) that allocated resources for implementing new general education programs.

[b]Percentages add to more than 100 percent due to multiple mentions.

were part of the new curriculum. Faculty trained in their own disciplines found it extraordinarily difficult to produce coherent courses that wove together several disciplines with a common theme.

On several campuses, the allocation of resources to promote communication with faculty was the hallmark of successful implementation. At the University of Minnesota, Morris the committee developing a freshman core course consulted extensively with the faculty before implementation. The committee made presentations to the faculty, held workshops on the readings, and developed a course guide. Faculty struggled with the philosophy and essence of the course and gave the committee substantial feedback. The course was refined and, upon implementation, was well understood by the faculty. At Bridgewater State a document called the "Green Book" was created to guide the faculty regarding the new general education program. This comprehensive book clearly presented the goals of the program and provided explicit guidelines for the inclusion criteria for courses. It became an invaluable resource for faculty.

In contrast, at the University of Massachusetts Boston almost no effort was made to educate the faculty about the goals that were to serve as the framework for each core course. Some who understood the goals simply did not know how to incorporate and work toward them. The program floundered for two years until the problems were addressed in a faculty handbook about the core program, and faculty seminars and colloquiums, supported by a Title III grant, were introduced.

Incentives for faculty to create new courses were another important part of resource allocation for general education programs. Two thirds of the campuses surveyed reported that such incentives were available on their campuses. At Seattle University, summer stipends were available for course development, and month-long seminars were held to update and improve course syllabi within the three "phases" of its core program. This support was found to be stimulating for the faculty and revitalizing for the curriculum.

Other campuses, such as the University of Maine at Machias, saw their interdisciplinary courses weaken when funds for course development evaporated. Given the already heavy load of teaching, advising, and community service, faculty had little time (or incentive) to devote to the development of new courses or new themes for existing interdisciplinary courses.

Finally, about half of the campuses reported that they had hired new faculty to help cover the demand for general education courses. Additional faculty were sometimes required to handle newly created courses (especially skills courses and interdisciplinary courses), not all of which could be staffed given the existing commitments of the faculty.

Aside from the sheer volume of courses to be staffed, however, there existed other problems—namely, negative incentives for faculty to teach in the general education program.

First, some faculty already had a heavy load of remedial and introductory courses. Teaching in the general education program often meant that they had to give up one or two upper-division courses (typically the most enjoyable ones). At Bridgewater State, for example, this negative incentive existed for the development of courses to satisfy the non-Western heritage requirement. Faculty hesitated to develop courses to fulfill the requirement because such courses were taught at an introductory level. Faculty members would have to give up an upper-division offering to teach yet another lower-level course.

Second, the reward system did not support faculty participation in the general education program. Generally departments made the recommendations for promotion and tenure—recommendations usually supported by upper levels of administration. General education courses taught outside the department (i.e., the interdisciplinary ones) were not valued at department review time because they did not contribute to the department. Similarly, the reward system did not support departmental participation in the general education program. That is, departments themselves typically received no credit for their faculty's teaching of general education courses outside the department.

The use of adjunct faculty in the general education program was commonly practiced for economic reasons but generally viewed as a poor solution. Full-time faculty, feeling overloaded, wanted permanent teaching slots created. The quality of teaching among adjuncts was uneven. Finally, the use of adjunct faculty in general education tended to diffuse the spirit of the program because the adjuncts were not versed in the philosophy and goals of the program.

For those campuses with no resources to hire new faculty, the inevitable shift in resources to cover general education became a bitter pill for some faculty. Existing courses had to be sacrificed so that faculty could be reassigned to interdisciplinary or core courses. For other campuses, such as Colby-

Sawyer, this shift may have saved some faculty slots at a time when enrollments were waning. For still other campuses, such as Plymouth State, upper-division courses suffered as faculty were reassigned to teach introductory-level general education courses.

Class size, too, became an issue on many campuses because of the resource and staffing constraints. In an effort to move students through the general education program, class size was frequently increased. This often decreased the effectiveness of the courses (especially writing courses) and resulted in animosity on the part of faculty, some of whom were already feeling aggrieved. Several campuses reported having size limits for general education courses, but according to faculty these limits were often ignored.

PROGRAMMATIC OUTCOMES

With few exceptions, general education programs became more structured entities after the attention given to them by the reform process. On two thirds (67 percent) of the campuses, programs became modified distribution systems. In such systems the number of courses that could be taken to fulfill requirements was dramatically reduced, and a few courses were required of all students. Almost half of the institutions (44 percent) required students to take interdisciplinary courses. On about one fifth of the campuses (22 percent) modified core programs were put into place. In these programs the majority of courses that students must take was specified, and students had the freedom to choose courses in only a few areas. Only 12 percent of the campuses retained a loose distribution system in which students had complete freedom of choice.

The change process was indeed perilous for all these institutions in a time of scarcity and insecurity. Poor planning, structural constraints, lack of resources, and passionate individual philosophies of general education all created tremendous barriers to the development of a single, coherent program.

The Politics of Curriculum Reform

The debate over general education became
somewhat entangled with empire building.
—FACULTY MEMBER, JOHNSON STATE COLLEGE

The previous chapters provide ample evidence that colleges and universities—even those with limited resources, less selective student bodies, and a brief history with the liberal arts—devote extraordinary effort to reforming their general education curricula. Clearly institutions that undertake curriculum change expect success, not failure. Yet, for all the good intentions focused on general education, the programs often achieve less than what their designers envisaged. In addition, the legacy of change at some campuses has been bitter. The process has exposed nerves lying just below an institution's skin. It has also exposed concerns remote from students' education. Some observers have arrived at the troubling realization that general education programs are conceived not in terms of the students at all; rather, general education seems to be primarily for and about the faculty.

As the focus on general education spread from the national arena to the local scene, local considerations became increasingly important. The transition from rhetoric to reality added a decidedly political dimension to the picture. As Harold D. Lasswell (1936) pointed out long ago, this raises questions of "who gets what, when, how."

ORGANIZATIONAL STRUCTURE AND POLITICS

Academics and observers of U.S. higher education have long grasped that organizational politics plays a role in college and university life. This is politics of a particular type, or, more accurately, types, since there is much variety in higher education. Although they do not tell the whole story, the organizational structures of colleges and universities provide clues to their politics. An organizational structure reveals formalized social relationships among various actors in the institution, defining who holds what formal power and how this power can be used (e.g., Arnold, 1994; Baldridge, 1971; Pfeffer, 1981).

In most colleges and universities, power is decentralized, spread across various constituencies that have loosely coupled ties with one another. The precise proportional distribution of power among faculty, administration, students, and trustees varies with the institution. This power mix at the individual campus needs to be understood when designing and implementing general education reform. Unless power is decisively skewed in favor of one constituency, which is rare, a unilateral approach to curriculum change can lead to gridlock and sometimes to outright rebellion.

The diffusion of power on campuses is sometimes offered as an argument for giving innovators sweeping authority. The interlocking social patterns in the organizational structure of colleges and universities are resistant to change, at least in the short term. Although a campus crisis provides an opportunity to reorganize, under normal conditions it is difficult for academic organizations to institute and apply the top-down management style so typical of traditional business corporations. This is why the secret design committee at Green Mountain College failed.

In addition to clues that the organizational structure provides about the political system of a campus there are the unofficial and sometimes less obvious attitudes, norms, and beliefs on a campus. Anyone seeking change must reckon with these powerful agents.[1] For example, campus customs, even if they are not spelled out in official documents, often dictate that various individuals or bodies should be consulted before a change. It is the act of consultation itself that is important. Ignoring such customs is usually a mistake. Those who believe they should be consulted and are not can impede the acceptance of a plan, even if they basically agree with the proposal. Ideas are judged not only for themselves but also for the way in which they are presented (Edelman, 1964; Feldman, 1989). Once colleges and universities are viewed as polities, this point seems axiomatic. Yet, however obvious it seems, the point is often missed in practice.

Some leaders on the campuses visited in this study appreciated the political ramifications of what they were taking on in attempting to reform general education. Many, however, overlooked the importance of local politics. Schools often entered the process with the idea that they were embarking on an important project; yet they conceived it narrowly. Like the proverbial iceberg in the waters of national concern about undergraduate education, the part above the surface—the curriculum—was what they saw. The part of the iceberg below the surface—other organizational factors to which general education is inevitably connected—was less apparent.

GENERAL EDUCATION AND ORGANIZATIONAL ISSUES

One important finding is that the process of design and implementation of general education often raises issues beyond those of what and how students should learn. Many faculty and administrators passionately believe in the importance of providing the best general education curriculum that circumstances will allow. While the rhetoric focuses on general education, other issues are present. These other issues can be interpreted as subtexts to the official project of curriculum change. Sometimes the issues are as obvious as the parochial concerns of a given department; at other times, debate about a general education curriculum provides an opportunity for larger issues to emerge, ones affecting the entire campus.

Political Subtexts

There are two types of political subtexts to change: those involving established units or individuals and those involving marginal units or individuals. First, certain issues affect the relationships of established organizational units to one another. The issues can also be related to the overall survival of the individual or of the campus in its larger environment. Such issues include general education as a way of maintaining or increasing departmental enrollments, of saving faculty jobs, and of giving the admissions department a program it can sell. At Colby-Sawyer, for example, the faculty's discussions of the general education curriculum became intertwined with their concern about maintaining their jobs. Enrollments had declined from more than 700 students in 1976 to 400 a decade later (although by 1991 more than 600 were enrolled). Declining enrollment brought in its wake a reduced faculty, partly through attrition, partly through terminations (see Box 4–1).

A second type of subtext to general education reform involves struggles for power by newer voices to attain recognition. This subtext is less dependent on the traditional campus units of organization.

Untangling these two subtexts is difficult. They tend to be entwined with conflicts among faculty cohorts. The faculty's power and prestige are associated with age or years of service. The typical faculty-ranking system—assistant professor, as-

BOX 4–1   Close-up: Colby-Sawyer College

Founded a century and a half ago in mid-state New London, New Hampshire, Colby-Sawyer College has had a long history of organizational change. Originally the New London Academy, a private coeducational secondary school, the institution in 1928 became the Colby Junior College for Women. Although it retained an emphasis on a two-year course of studies, by 1943 the college was also offering fledgling baccalaureate programs. In 1975, the school was renamed yet again, as Colby-Sawyer College, and in 1989 the trustees voted to readmit men.

In the 1970s the general education portion of the curriculum was a loosely organized system of distribution requirements. Many faculty were dissatisfied with the core program's menu approach. Between the mid-1970s and 1980 such groups as the Curriculum and Instruction Committee discussed a common education for Colby-Sawyer students. In 1979, the president established an internal discussion and planning group, the Committee for the 80s, to examine the entire institution, including its curriculum. A consultant visited the college as part of the activities of one of the committee's subgroups (on liberal learning). Soon thereafter the consultant was appointed provost and helped prompt more thinking about the issue.

During the early to mid-1980s the campus in general grappled with the issue of whether the college should focus somewhat more on vocational education or, more strictly, on the liberal arts. By fall 1982 several small groups had been formed to deal with a core program—not for developing models for a core curriculum but, rather, for discussing and generating ideas. All faculty members and many administrators were members of one of these

(Continued)

BOX 4–1   *(Continued)*

groups; care was taken to ensure that groups did not have more than one member from the same department. Each group produced a set of notions believed to be imperative for a liberal education.

In spring 1983 the entire faculty met in a series of evening meetings to synthesize the work of the small groups. One observer described the process as "discussion and vote, discussion and vote." Some disagreed about the path Colby-Sawyer should take, and, in the end, compromises were made in the name of expediency. For example, in return for its participation in the core, one department insisted on being assigned upper-level students and on team teaching. Nevertheless, through this process the faculty arrived at something new that started out with "no strikes against it." The design was based upon two areas of broad agreement. First, all Colby-Sawyer students would share a common core of learning. Second, this learning was to be achieved through an interdisciplinary approach. The core proposals covered fine and performing arts, natural sciences, social sciences, the humanities, and health sciences. The final design, consisting of five core courses along with core electives, was voted on in late spring 1983, and the plan was adopted for the 1983/84 academic year.

According to observers, the plan's implementation took place in a heavily politicized atmosphere, no small part of which was probably the result of enrollment difficulties that were fueling retrenchment. One faculty member recalled a strong desire of faculty to make no changes that would lead to the loss of students studying in any given department.

The new plan's implementation was left to individual departments. No separate budget was in place for the creation of core courses, and, as late as 1991, budgets for

BOX 4–1 *(Continued)*

core courses were still embedded in otherwise undifferentiated departmental budgets. Even senior administrators did not know what the program was actually costing. Questions of staffing and how core courses would be taught were given little attention. Operational course designs for each of the identified core areas were needed. Thus many decisions had yet to be made. The implementation phase became, in effect, an extension of the design phase. One observer noted that core courses were changed more or less "as we saw fit—sometimes no one really gave approval or noticed." One administrator suggested that more coordination among departments would have prevented problems. Another, however, suggested that working through this process—almost by trial and error—was a necessary step.

In anticipation of an accreditation visit a review was made of the general education program beginning in 1992. As a result the health and wellness requirement was dropped, the number of electives in arts and sciences was increased, and a senior capstone requirement was added. The program was modified in 1993 to include a proficiency requirement in computer literacy and a first-year colloquium entitled "Transition to College Life."

sociate professor, and professor—reflects the distribution of political power. Striving for the protection and privileges of tenure, assistant professors are in a weak position compared to senior professors.

Beyond generational conflict, campuses also struggle with the place of women and ethnic and racial minorities in the academy. More females and minorities have joined the faculty, clustering at lower levels. Thus, what might be considered a normal conflict between the old guard and the new guard is more complex than age differences.

Lines of Demarcation

When conflicts emerge, both substantive issues and the people involved need to be considered. Often a correlation exists between one's position in the organization and the policies one favors. For example, Morton Halperin (1974) noted that, although all members of the Department of Defense and the Pentagon presumably subscribed to similar goals for defense policies in the 1960s, specific proposals were colored by what he termed "grooved thinking," or the tendency "to focus on a few key variables and to have a programmed response to those particular variables," often according to "organizational interests" defined by the affiliations of individuals with certain units (p. 23).

Not every actor in a college or university department feels the same kinship and loyalties. Still, all faculty members are located in a division, department, or program. When the views and policies traditionally associated with this unit are not shared by a person occupying it, conflict arises. The contest is often framed in terms of "traditionalists" and "modernists," who are predisposed to reject the "grooved thinking" in their subunits.

Although varying according to local circumstances, the conflict surrounding general education change can be understood in two ways: conflict among established interests and conflict between emerging and established interests.

LEGITIMACY AND RESOURCES

Organizational politics enters the picture when differing views about what general education should be, from a philosophical level, are joined to organizational issues, subtexts, and lines of demarcation. The internal politics fall along two dimensions. First is the *politics of legitimacy,* which entails the struggle among organizational units to attain or maintain a level of prestige on campus. Second is the *politics of resource allocation,* in which units struggle for funding, students, and other tangible privileges.

The Politics of Legitimacy

The design of a general education program sets the stage for academic units to struggle for legitimacy and compete for prestige. General education seems an unlikely drama, especially since general education sometimes appears to be an unwanted enterprise that does not fit neatly into the disciplinary or professional emphases of today's colleges and universities. Thus it seems paradoxical that a matter of legitimacy is associated with it. As an observer at one campus noted, although general education tends to have a meager reputation among many faculty, every department wants to be included as part of it.

In part, academic units may be competing for scarce resources. It is doubtful, however, that all struggles over general education can be reduced to that. Rather, general education provides a vehicle in which the legitimacy of an academic unit—or an entire institution, for that matter—can be rehearsed symbolically, allowing the prestige of various members of an academic community to be announced and reaffirmed.

At the University of Maine at Machias a struggle emerged along lines of academic affiliation. On the one hand were faculty from professional programs, such as education and business, who favored the campus's traditional mission of serving community and regional needs by preparing students for employment. On the other hand were faculty, usually newer arrivals on campus, in traditional arts and sciences departments who thought that a new general education program should serve the goal of transforming the campus into a small liberal arts college. Thus a major part of the politics surrounding general education was between two camps divided according to divisional and departmental affiliation.

In addition, the politics of legitimacy appears to work against the establishment of discrete general education departments, with attendant consequences for the prestige of new and existing general education programs. Since general education is often delivered through departments, the director of general education, if there is one, is often a shepherd tending someone else's flock. The results are mixed. At the University of Massachusetts Boston, for example, where departments had authority over the core curriculum courses in their areas, the university committee overseeing the core had difficulty monitoring the program and ensuring its quality. In departments where general education received low priority or where core teaching was weak, the oversight committee had no leverage to improve the program because the courses "belonged" to the departments. Official faculty reviews for promotion, tenure, and merit pay were outside the jurisdiction of the oversight committee. The lack of real authority was evidence of the lesser legitimacy and prestige of the oversight committee as compared with the established departments.

The decision-making process in designing a new general education program can itself be a source of conflict. The degree of legitimacy accorded to that process and to the people participating in it has important implications for the ultimate acceptance of the new plan. At Green Mountain College, for example, the initial design committee resembled a grand jury. Only after the designers had a full picture of their idea for a new curriculum did they communicate officially with the faculty at large. The committee had insufficiently recognized serious doubts about the legitimacy of the closed process. Not surprisingly, the proposal failed to win approval.

In contrast, the decision-making processes at Colby-Sawyer College and Bridgewater State College were open and inclusive and seen to be legitimate. A valuable byproduct of openness and inclusiveness was noticeably greater satisfaction among faculty and administrators with the redesigned general education program. The sense of community at these schools was enhanced, rather than diminished.

The politics of legitimacy is similarly apparent in struggles over whose voices are included in the curriculum. For example, at the University of Massachusetts Boston, an effort to change general education in the late 1970s cast what some sources called "'60s'radicals" against their older, more traditional colleagues. Radicals and traditionalists in such departments as English, philosophy, history, economics, political science, and fine arts, as well as a few from psychology, sociology, and anthropology, split in their support of general education changes, most often along ideological lines.[2] From the radical perspective it was the radicals who, according to one campus observer, "cared about pedagogy . . . as opposed to those who see the university as a place for academic experts." The now familiar conflict between the sexes was similarly apparent at some of the campuses visited. It had originally been part of the story at the University of Maine at Machias, although that aspect was soon overshadowed by divisional conflict. It was also evident at Albertus Magnus College, where, by the late 1970s, faculty sympathetic to feminism and liberation ideologies were struggling to legitimate new points of view. Mirroring the new perspectives, the general education program was seen as a place in the curriculum that should be receptive to gender and racial issues. This created a situation in which political philosophies and friendships became determinants of faculty attitudes about the program. Traditional disciplinary alliances were therefore minimized (see Box 4–2).

Finally, the politics of legitimacy can influence the implementation of a new general education program. If those charged with implementing a plan perceive it as lacking legitimacy, the new program can wither. At the University of Massachusetts Boston, for example, four factors hindered the implementation of its revised curriculum in the early 1980s. First, many

BOX 4–2   Close-up: Albertus Magnus College

Albertus Magnus College is a Catholic college in New Haven, Connecticut. The faculty represent a wide range of outlooks. Although surprising to some, diversity of viewpoints is increasingly a fact of life in Catholic colleges and universities.

By the late 1970s, Albertus Magnus faculty had become increasingly disenchanted with the existing general education program, which was then a loose system of distribution requirements. The faculty created a task force to review general education. One result was the creation of an innovative program called "Modes of Inquiry." The philosophy behind this program was that general education should emphasize not the specific content of academic disciplines but intellectual skills, encouraging faculty from various disciplinary backgrounds to work together. The plan called for paired courses in which a single critical skill and a single core topic would be explored from two disciplinary perspectives. In one example a sociologist was to be teamed with a social historian to teach a pair of courses on the topic of technology. To ensure coordination, the faculty members were to sit in on each other's class and collaborate on the two-course syllabi.

Although the plan may have appeared straightforward, in practice, Modes of Inquiry proved divisive, contributing to a "canonical battle" on campus, according to one observer. The faculty became largely fractionalized, with one camp strongly supporting the program and the other strongly opposed to it. Efforts to insert the philosophies of the emergent voices placed some faculty in diametric opposition to the traditional, discipline-bound attitudes of senior faculty.

In 1985, the situation became further complicated. Declining enrollments led this women's college to adopt

BOX 4–2 *(Continued)*

coeducation. Partly as a consequence of this change the college president asked the faculty to select eight people for a "consolidation" committee to make the college's educational program more efficient. A subcommittee to review general education was created. It consisted of two female members perceived as conservative and two men thought to be strong supporters of the Modes initiative.

Perceptions can be inaccurate. As it turned out, the two men were actually much more moderate in their commitment to the program than had been assumed. The men provided the middle ground between the "progressive" faculty, who rallied around Modes, and more traditional faculty. Acting as mediators, the men were instrumental in hammering out a revised general education plan that preserved some ideas from Modes but included discipline-based distributional ideas.

The polarization over the curriculum created during the time that Modes of Inquiry was in effect had by then taken its toll on the faculty. The revised general education plan, emphasizing compromise between the two poles, was quickly accepted by the faculty and approved by the board of trustees.

faculty simply did not know what the program was aiming at with its goal of introducing students "to the concepts and methods of a broad area of knowledge" (as opposed to a discipline-based conception); further, they were uncertain about how to introduce the then emerging idea of critical thinking into their core courses. Second, some of those who understood the aims of the new curriculum were nevertheless uncertain about how to combine the goals of the curriculum into a single course. These two problems could have been solved with more attention to the faculty's understanding of the program. The other two factors were thornier. Some faculty members thought from the beginning that the goals of the new curriculum would be impossible to achieve in the same course. These faculty apparently had no intention of participating. Other faculty simply did not believe in the goals of the changes. Thus cooperation in the implementation of the new curriculum was severely undermined from the outset by the views of some faculty that the new plan was more or less impossible or unwise and, hence, not legitimate.

The Politics of Resource Allocation

The competition for legitimacy may be associated with the struggle for resources because resources are allocated primarily to those perceived as legitimate. Within an organization the amount of resources allocated to the parts is often commensurate with the prestige of those parts. The struggle for legitimacy sometimes involves more fundamental issues, such as simple recognition and affirmation of what one is already doing. Still, the competition for scarce resources, especially in colleges and universities with limited resources, is perhaps a more straightforward catalyst for political behavior in general education reform.

When change is being implemented, the presence or absence of resources often determines how well, if at all, proposals are carried out. Some of the schools in this study examined the question of resources when designing a new general education program; others neglected it. Even among those that explicitly considered resources a disjunction often emerged between the intention to fund a new program expressed in the design phase and the actual availability of resources when the time came to implement proposals.

One aspect of the politics of resource allocation can be located between administrators, who control the purse strings, and faculty bodies officially charged with overseeing the implementation of a new curriculum. It is the rare senior administrator who does not enthusiastically endorse the idea of a revised general education program. By the time of implementation, however, for a variety of reasons, these same people are unable to allocate sufficient resources for fulfilling this goal.

The initial funding for changing general education sometimes included grant money from outside agencies interested in improving undergraduate education. When this funding expired, the subsequent commitment to continue funding aspects of the projects—such as faculty seminars and workshops and release time for faculty working on developing and implementing new general education courses—varied widely. For example, at Johnson State College, when a Title III grant that had provided course releases for faculty who taught interdisciplinary courses expired, the number of such courses dropped significantly. In another college a new curriculum, not markedly different from the college's existing practice, was created for general education and was enthusiastically received by the faculty. Part of the original design called for a full-time general education director to oversee the program. There was a lag in the creation of this position, and then it was funded on a part-time basis. Even after the new curriculum had been in place for several years, the provost did not know what resources had been allocated to the program. Seven years after adoption of the new curriculum, steps were being initiated to determine what resources the program was using and to establish a separate budget for general education. Because departments were delegated responsibility for implementing general education courses, resource allocations for general education were subsumed into departmental budgets. Nobody seemed to know what this new curriculum was costing the college. This situation was by no means unique, showing how the political weakness of general education programs can result in less than optimal implementation decisions.

Academic units sometimes assume that their inclusion in a general education program will lead to the apportionment of additional resources. Sometimes the existence of new general education requirements appears to have ensured the continued funding of departments that were languishing. This was the case at some campuses where professionally or vocationally oriented programs were displacing traditional humanities study. More frequently hopes for additional resources were dashed. Many on campus complained that the resources available were insufficiently increased—if increased at all—to do the job of general education well.

The tangible costs of developing actual courses are sometimes underestimated. For example, at the University of Bridgeport (Box 4–3), funding was obtained from the National Endowment for the Humanities to develop four interdisciplinary courses. Only two such courses were developed sufficiently to be taught. When offered, enrollments were low, and the courses were subsequently dropped. Although other issues may have played a part, the important point is that rather than being reworked into viable courses, which would have meant expenditure of university money, the courses were eliminated altogether.

Some administrations believed that the faculty would develop, gratis, the courses required for new general education programs. This assumption was somewhat unrealistic, especially in cases, such as Johnson State College, in which a set of interdisciplinary courses was planned. Such courses, existing by definition outside the normative discipline-bound orientations and interests of faculty, were unlikely candidates to be developed without additional resources. The usual practice of colleges and universities is to reward faculty for research and departmentally oriented teaching as well as service. Without separate funding, or without a restructuring of the reward system itself, the costs of developing nontraditional or nondepartmental courses are shifted to faculty who choose to develop them. The issue is not only costs in money but also costs in time and effort. Faculty who devote their energies to designing innovative courses are unavailable for other activities

BOX 4–3   Close-up: University of Bridgeport

First established in 1927 as a junior college, the University of Bridgeport, a private, comprehensive university, gained four-year university status two decades later. It confers degrees from an associate in arts (A.A.) to a doctorate of education (Ed.D.). The university in 1988 had an enrollment of 5,345, half of whom were part-time students and more than half of whom were undergraduates. At that time the university, with a faculty of 428, had a School of Law (since departed) and four colleges: Arts and Humanities, Business and Public Management, Health and Human Services, and Science and Engineering. In addition, the university offered Metropolitan College, a continuing education program for part-time graduate and undergraduate students.

The headlines of the 1960s and early 1970s—with burgeoning enrollments, especially in the liberal arts—encouraged the institution to become a major regional university. It embarked on an ambitious plan of investment: new plant, new equipment, new faculty, new programs. By the mid-1970s, however, problems arose. Students were forsaking the liberal arts for preprofessional programs; women were expanding their career options beyond traditional professions, like teaching and nursing; more students were choosing majors in business, engineering, and health sciences—all contributing to the loss of popularity of the liberal arts and education courses at the university. Of equal significance, competition for students intensified as other regional colleges began to attract a larger share of the applicant pool. The university's enrollment plateaued in this period and then began a steady decline.

The modestly endowed university had borrowed from

(Continued)

BOX 4–3   *(Continued)*

local banks to finance its expansion. The decline in enrollments—and the consequent loss of tuition monies—reduced the revenue stream. Initiating university-wide cost cutting, the administration discharged part-time instructional staff, prompting the heavily tenured faculty to unionize. Three strikes ensued.

Before the financial crises, Bridgeport's students had only one university-wide required course, Freshman Composition. The individual colleges determined other general education requirements for their students. Unhappy with this situation, the administration urged the development of a core curriculum based on the model adopted by Harvard. In 1973, the Andrew W. Mellon Foundation granted $500,000 to establish a fund, the income of which was to foster humanities education. Then, in 1975, the National Endowment for the Humanities sponsored a consultant, who two years later recommended a nontraditional format of innovative interdisciplinary offerings.

Over the next few years three Core Commissions were established to develop, refine, and implement a university-wide general education program. In 1978, the first commission outlined a three-part framework for a core curriculum: (1) a skills section (writing, oral communication, quantitative and logical analyses, research techniques), (2) subject matter (personal, physical, and collective environments; man's shaping spirit; historical perspectives), and (3) shared intellectual experience (a great-issues approach). Charged with developing specific plans for the core curriculum, the second commission in 1979 proposed a three-component program: basic skills, "Heritage" courses (interdisciplinary approaches to the humanities and to social and natural sciences), and a capstone seminar. It spelled out the credit hours required for each kind of degree, the distribution and kinds of

---

BOX 4–3   *(Continued)*

courses in each component, and the administrative me-
chanics of the curriculum. The third commission oversaw
implementation of the core curriculum. During implementation much of the interdisciplinary emphasis and even
the writing-intensive character of the Heritage component were lost.

The general education program, the Core, enjoyed
limited success. Yet an observation about the program
made in 1987 was a telling one: "Few faculty or students
are enthusiastic about UB's core curriculum . . . [they]
have learned to live with it. . . ."

By the end of the 1980s the central question was not,
however, the quality of a student's liberal education but
the university's survival. The school was saved from bankruptcy in 1992 through funding from the Professors World
Peace Academy, an organization associated with the Uni-
fication Church. By then many of the faculty responsible
for getting the new general education program off the
ground had lost their jobs.

---

potentially more likely to lead to recognition and rewards, such
as tenure.

The resource question has other manifestations. Existing disciplinary departments view the obligation to teach general education courses as drawing attention away from majors. There is a struggle to balance these competing needs
within departments. At one campus, when too few faculty volunteered to teach the department's general education courses,
the department chair assigned this duty to department members who were unwilling, unprepared, or unenthusiastic about
teaching them.

Some chairs are unconvinced that their best faculty should be teaching general education courses. Others appear to have given little thought about who teaches in general education programs. The temptation to rely on part-time personnel for this purpose is great, as is the temptation to negotiate with the dean's office for favors in return for delivering the requested number of sections in a semester. Some department chairs do try earnestly to work with the general education program. However, the placement of general education teaching assignments in the hands of department chairs makes it possible for the politics of resource allocation to be played out both within the department (as with the decision of whom to assign to a given course) and between the departments and the dean's office.

When resources are scarce, as they increasingly are, the competition among organizational entities can overshadow consideration of general education needs. Unrealistic assumptions about the resources available for general education generally benefit the more powerful, more established organizational units and are detrimental to those aspects of a general education curriculum that are extraneous to, or counter to, those interests.

Conflicts in General Education Change

The politics of legitimacy and the politics of resource allocation have been played out, in general, across the campuses. Some campuses have been able to deal successfully with conflicts emerging throughout the change process, although this has sometimes meant settling for less than the desired degree of change in general education. On other campuses, conflict has erupted in a damaging way and contaminated the change process sufficiently to undermine it.

The case of Albertus Magnus College reveals how the resolution of conflict can have consequences for a general education program. Traditional views of general education were challenged by those faculty who were sympathetic to newer ideological perspectives and who were open to circumventing the usual departmental perspective. At first the faculty split into two camps. Yet, when asked by the college president to reevaluate the college's educational programs, faculty devised and quickly adopted a compromise.

That compromise was no small achievement. The college's declining fortunes resulted both in coeducation and in a moratorium on tenure. Faculty were asked to review the college educational program with a view toward consolidating it in the light of coeducation. The moratorium highlighted the tenuousness of faculty job security and may have contributed to a climate in which emerging voices—many of whom lacked tenure at the time of the moratorium—found themselves in a weakened position.

Albert O. Hirschman (1970) observed that the choices open to individuals in such circumstances are what he called "exit," "voice," and "loyalty" (p. 38). In the introduction of coeducation and retrenchment caused by the tenure moratorium, *voice,* or active opposition to the organization's prevailing order, was a potentially dangerous course of action for untenured faculty. In the period following these changes a number of faculty chose to *exit* the college. Those who remained chose something like *loyalty,* or at least a willingness to compromise, as the most viable option. The seeming ease with which compromise was reached in 1985 was a function of the larger context of change that the college faced. In such uncertainty, interests corresponding to the established order on campus had the upper hand.

ATTENTION TO CONTEXT

Most of the difficulty in creating new general education programs seems to revolve around reaching agreement on a philosophical level about what such a curriculum should include and what a student should know. The creation and implementation of a new curriculum, however, raise issues beyond this, some closely related and others more remote. This situation is reminiscent of the "organized anarchy" that is said to result sometimes in "garbage-can" decision-making processes (e.g., Cohen, March, & Olsen, 1972; Kingdon, 1984; March & Olsen, 1979).[3] In this conception, "choice opportunities," that is, situations in which decisions must be made, can involve a confluence of three organizational "streams." The first stream is that of the problems themselves—for example, the problem of how to reform a general education curriculum. The second organizational stream is the stream of potential solutions, which may actually predate the problems to which they become attached in a decision-making process. Policies envisioned originally for one purpose may come to be offered as the answer to a wholly different problem. The final stream is that of the individual's participation in the decision-making process. This is another way of saying that attention to a problem, or the lack of it, influences the decision. Because of the many combinations and permutations of these streams from one campus to another it is not surprising that the study found highly variable patterns of participation in decision-making processes (Cohen, March, & Olsen, 1972; March & Olsen, 1989).

On a broader level, many facets of organizational life in colleges and universities are institutionalized and not easily changed (Powell, 1988; Zucker, 1983, 1988). This study found that the way in which organizational units, such as offices and departments, interact is among the most institutionalized aspects of academic organization. For this reason, such fundamental organizational activities as general education cannot be considered in isolation, without reference to the organization as a whole. As previously noted, two dimensions become part of such curriculum change. First are issues associated with the politics of legitimacy; second, those associated with the politics of resource allocation, which are perhaps more visible. Yet underlying issues of legitimacy and prestige weigh heavily in curriculum change because they profoundly affect the members of the academy who must carry out such change—the faculty. That conflict can become part of general education change is therefore not unexpected. Conflict may indeed be inevitable.

Much attention has been focused nationally on the philosophical merits of various approaches to general education and the undergraduate curriculum. The discourse tends to consider general education as a self-contained entity. The logic of general education reform, however, lies both within proposed changes and in the relationship between proposed changes and the organization. This research suggests that greater attention to the nuances of the individual campus—its structure, beliefs, and normative practices—is necessary to bring about general education reform.

NOTES

1. See John W. Meyer and Brian Rowan, "Institutionalized Organizations: Formal Structure as Myth and Ceremony" (1977), and Lynne G. Zucker, "Institutional Theories of Organizations" (1987).

2. Faculty in various science departments were not so identified. Following Morton Halperin's (1974) notion of grooved thinking, a plausible explanation may be that those trained in the natural sciences deal largely with issues outside the sphere of human organization. Questions of what group holds power or dictates the way in which human problems are viewed and investigated, although important to humanistic or social science inquiries, are less relevant to investigations in chemistry, physics, and so forth.

3. The negative connotations of the terms "organized anarchy" and "garbage-can decision making" are unfortunate because they inadvertently obscure the genuine interconnectedness and value of many facets of organizational life.

▶ 5

Culture and
Community

*Perhaps there is no curriculum . . . only an
assumption of burdens and discrete programs
for carrying them out, an accidental compromise between the only partially understood
past and the unanticipated future.*
—*FREDERICK RUDOLPH (1977, p. 24)*

In many discussions of the influence of the environment on
general education reform, colleges and universities are seen
as entrepreneurial actors responding to a variety of immediate market factors. Chapter 2 presents essentially this view.
Another view sees the academy as highly resistant to change
because of political struggles that lead to gridlock. Chapter 4
examines this view. Yet something is missing. Neither a market framework nor a political one can account for the matrix
of sentiments, beliefs, and values that drives the process of
changing a general education curriculum. A cultural explanation that takes actors' meanings and concerns as a central unit
of analysis contributes to such an understanding. A chief advantage of such an approach is that it allows one to discern
meanings and concerns that are less visible—and sometimes

nonrational—but that affect the nature and course of institutional change. Culture is complex and paradoxical, and any account of it must operate at several levels.

A caution is in order, however, for cultural analysis obscures the necessity for colleges to respond to market conditions (e.g., new student populations) and authority structures (e.g., state boards of higher education). These forces have consequences in the cultural world that themselves contribute to the shaping of culture. In short, market forces, political processes, and cultural phenomena influence one another and are disentangled only for analytic purposes.

This chapter looks at three institutions—two public and one private—that inaugurated imaginative new general education curricula: Seattle University, an urban, medium-size, private Jesuit campus; the University of Massachusetts Boston, a large urban university; and the University of Minnesota, Morris, a small, residential, rural liberal arts college that bills itself as a "public ivy." Notwithstanding their differences, these institutions are similar in several respects. First, each has experienced economic contraction, either in the recent past or in the present. Second, as part of its "survival formula" each attempted to make itself distinctive through its general education program. Third, in this effort each obtained external funds, whether from private foundations or the federal government. A fourth motivation intersected fundamentally with the local culture and even with the faculty's personal longings. That motivation, or subtext, was the quest for community in the face of social change.

Since the late 1960s higher education has become increasingly complex. New groups have entered the nation's classrooms, bringing with them new backgrounds and needs. Ethnic, racial, and gender studies and other interest groups, all containing an impulse for the redress of social and political grievances, have come to dot the collegiate landscape. Traditional attitudes about how education should proceed are questioned and revised, with much talk of learning communities, critical thinking, writing across the curriculum, competency-based education, and other innovations. Faculty and administrative roles have been redefined—all in a period of dwindling resources, which has led to greater centralization of power in the administration and split faculty communities. These changes have been duly noted, time and again, in conferences and publications about higher education. "Change," reported one faculty member, "is not only in the air, it's in the *Chronicle*."

Given these circumstances and the prominence accorded them in the national as well as higher education media, it is not surprising to hear of a yearning for community. Indeed, it is symptomatic that people have been thinking in terms of the *intentional* building of community. Said simply, if communities consist of people who tell the same stories, campuses consist increasingly of people—students, faculty, and administrators—who are telling very different stories.[1]

On the campuses visited the design and implementation of a new general education program became inexorably bound up with the attempt to tell a mutually acceptable, encompassing story of the world—or at least of what the college stood for in the world—even if the story had to be bargained over. To understand this process requires a close look at the inner culture of higher education.

IDEAL AND REAL CULTURES OF INSTITUTIONS

Colleges, like all institutions, have an "ideal culture" and a "real culture." The former refers to the norms and values advocated in principle, the latter to those adhered to in practice.

Academic Community

On the campuses visited, one aspect of ideal culture, expressed in complex and varying ways, is that of academic community.

Few places thought they had it, although all longed for it, especially in the light of the campus's increasing fragmentation. At a deeper level, academic community supplies a connectedness to people that both reflects and supports serious learning. In this way, community satisfies the more primal needs of social existence: the cultivation and perpetuation of meaning, identity, predictability, and a sense of membership in a collectivity that is worth belonging to because it protects what its members value. It is to help satisfy such communal needs that all social institutions have shared knowledge, myths, traditions, folkways, in-jokes, rituals, ceremonies, festivals, lore, beliefs concerning outsiders, and systems of authority. Campuses are not exempted from this general rule. Campus life—learning itself—for many people is a profoundly communal experience, with many people acting in concert to make it happen. This is one way in which the American ethic of individual achievement conceals more than it reveals.

With general education reform as the vehicle, most campuses wanted and expected to build or reinvigorate a sense of community. It is not uncommon for academics, with their heightened messianic and utopian instincts, to want more. As chronicled by Gerald Grant and David Riesman in *The Perpetual Dream* (1978), reforms in higher education often embody purposes that are informed by idealistic, romantic, and even quasi-sacred values and moral codes. Such yearnings were demonstrated in the almost beatific and pastoral language of Ernest Boyer's call for a campus community in the Carnegie Foundation for the Advancement of Teaching's (1990) report on the campus experience. A campus community should, he stated, be purposeful, open, just, disciplined, caring, and celebratory.[2] The quest for community is, of course, a reflection of the American experience, from the Puritan "errand into the wilderness," with its own teleology, to today's search for some "practical ritual and moral 'structure' that orders our freedom and binds our choices into something like habits of the heart" (Bellah et al., 1985, p. 137).[3]

The notion of academic community itself may contain elements of the mythical. Perhaps "community" is a chimera, a pleasant word but an unreachable, outdated, inappropriate, or false ideal, yet one held onto nonetheless. Perhaps community consists not of people who tell one story but of people who—through strife, struggle, and reason—come to know one another's diverse stories. In any case, shared belief in a myth, however much it distorts reality, moves people to orient to the same object or symbols and, in so doing, is a unifying force (Smelser, 1987).

Correlates of Community

The largest and most structurally complex universities are generally the least likely to develop a coherent ethos or tone that would inform and sustain a sense of community. Yet a strict correlation between size and the development of community does not exist. Some small campuses in this study were racked with dissension, whereas medium-size Seattle University (see Box 5–1), with its religious tradition, had a unifying intellectual and moral tone. In the late 1960s and early 1970s,

---

BOX 5–1   Close-up: Seattle University

Founded in 1891, Seattle University consists of eight academic units: the College of Arts and Sciences, the Albers School of Business and Economics, Matteo Ricci College, the School of Education, the School of Law, the School of Nursing, the School of Science and Engineering, and the Graduate School. In 1990, Seattle enrolled approximately 3,000 undergraduates and 1,500 graduate students.

The 52-acre campus near the center of Seattle, Washington is filled with surprises. Winding paths, flower beds,

(Continued)

BOX 5–1   *(Continued)*

fountains, and a hanging garden cascading from a parking garage combine to give a tranquil, almost countryside feel to this overbuilt urban institution. However, this small private college has had its share of troubles. In the mid-1960s the Boeing Aircraft Company, the region's largest employer, cut its employment in half, sending the region into a cataclysmic decline and the college into near bankruptcy. The William Boeing Foundation rescued the school after it agreed to appoint a lay board of trustees and institute a moratorium on salaries, promotions, and new hires.

By 1980 the college was on much better footing. Enrollments were rising, spurred in part by the growing popularity of the Puget Sound area. Graduate and undergraduate programs in software engineering and international business were added to the roster of programs to appeal to students with a vocational bent. The university brought in new faculty to teach in professional programs.

The university's priority had traditionally been teaching. Especially in the College of Arts and Sciences, faculty were recruited for their teaching interests and abilities. Student contact was taken seriously. Faculty were expected to be on campus, teaching, five days a week. Some of the new faculty resisted the idea that they were teachers first and foremost and were averse to being on campus every day of the week. They wanted to do research and consulting.

Another change during the 1980s was the composition of the student body. By 1990, 20 percent of students were minorities and only about half were Catholic. Within the university, enrollments shifted as well, with most students now majoring in professional programs rather than the liberal arts. These changes reflected the general education debate that occurred on the Seattle campus.

BOX 5–1   *(Continued)*

A faculty member began the process by persuading a dean to set up a task force to review the college's general education curriculum. To everyone's surprise, he found a foundation willing to subsidize the university's planning process. A faculty committee, with membership open to anyone interested in working on general education reform, was given the go-ahead to design a university-wide general education reform. Central to the committee's efforts was a belief in the importance of Christian ethics, especially the value of service to others. Another key part of a Jesuit education was the learning of Aristotelian philosophy, critical thinking, and the acquisition of a broad liberal education.

An implementation grant from the same foundation provided additional funds. However, deans voiced concern that the committee's efforts had not yet crystallized into a coherent design. Everything seemed too fluid; ideas remained abstract. The committee responded to the criticisms by preparing a statement detailing the goals of the reform. Nonetheless, the deans remained concerned. Under pressure, the committee disbanded.

A new steering committee was formed, and a long-time faculty member was appointed to undertake fresh efforts. In three daylong workshops the community gathered to work out the details of the general education plan. By the end of the third day everyone at the workshop felt comfortable with the changes in the general education curriculum. An imaginative and ambitious new general education program had been hatched.

Students would now take courses in three broad areas of study: foundations of wisdom, studies of persons in society, and responsibility and service. The program interspersed core courses in ethics, theology, and philosophy

(Continued)

BOX 5–1   *(Continued)*

with a strong writing-across-the-curriculum program, cluster courses, and an emphasis on service and community. Although the process was not without controversy, faculty were generally pleased with the results. Since this program was instituted, Seattle University has continued to invest heavily in summer faculty-development workshops, and the core curriculum has emphasized social and political awareness.

---

during a deep regional recession, Seattle University had faced declining enrollments and near bankruptcy. Among many steps taken to save the institution during this period, a faculty committee was appointed to recommend changes in the curriculum structure. It was hoped that these changes would make the university more attractive to prospective students. With increasing competition from area colleges and universities, especially the University of Washington, faculty and administrators more than ever felt an urgency about defining a clearer identity for the university.

At the University of Massachusetts Boston (see Box 5–2), extensive bureaucratization, size, and academic specialization militated against the growth of a common culture across academic departments or schools. The one exception to this was the nucleus of arts and sciences faculty dedicated to the development of new teaching strategies. These faculty led the formation of the new general education curriculum; as a core of like-minded believers they found camaraderie and intellectual stimulation in one another's company. By setting itself apart as progressive and in the know, and by developing the new program quickly, this group became exclusionary and isolated. The results were counterproductive. The proportion of faculty who came to feel a sense of ownership of the curriculum—and

BOX 5–2   Close-up: University of Massachusetts Boston

The University of Massachusetts Boston was founded in 1965 as a branch of the state university. Unlike the sprawling flagship campus situated in the rural western reaches of the state, the campus of the University of Massachusetts Boston consists of a complex of brick towers built on a thin peninsula of land jutting into Dorchester Bay. People are protected by the bay's winter winds by glass-encased walkways that connect the towers and pass over an austere bluestone-and-brick courtyard.

The university offers undergraduate and graduate degrees in the liberal arts and sciences as well as in business, nursing, teaching, public and community service, and a variety of preprofessional and vocational fields. The approximately 10,500 undergraduates are ethnically and racially diverse, come from a 50-mile radius of the campus, and are usually the first in their families to go to college. Many enter college with deficiencies both in basic academic skills and in general education, as well as in study habits.

Initially the University of Massachusetts Boston had two liberal arts schools, Colleges I and II, each with a different conception of education and each with its distinctive general education curriculum. College I was relatively nonprescriptive in curriculum requirements, interdisciplinary and experimental. College II had a traditional ethos and, correspondingly, a more structured and sequential curriculum. In both colleges, however, faculty complained that many students were being graduated with great gaps in their liberal arts education, in addition to not knowing how to read and write well. This informal grumbling about general education led to a seminar

(Continued)

BOX 5–2 *(Continued)*

series, funded by the Ford Foundation and led by Charles Muscatine, a leading innovator at the University of California at Berkeley, on designing a core curriculum. In these seminars a program was roughed out, including reading, writing, mathematics, and critical-thinking skills, followed by considerable discussion about how to teach them.

However fertile the ground for change, the real impetus came from the state. Severe budget cuts during 1976–1978 prompted the merger of Colleges I and II into the College of Arts and Sciences, and with that arose the need to develop quickly one general education curriculum. Three years later another merger occurred. In the summer of 1981 the state legislature and governor mandated the merger of Boston State College with the University of Massachusetts Boston. Faculty were divided between those who wanted somehow to combine the two disparate curricula and those who wanted to develop or at least to explore the possibility of a core curriculum, an idea to which they had so recently been exposed through the Ford Foundation–sponsored seminars.

The final arrangements were mired in difficulty. From the beginning, support for the curriculum was never wide enough to ensure its viability or to prevent its disintegration into a disconnected array of miscellaneous courses. Nor was there an appropriate administrative apparatus to run it on a daily basis. The willingness to pioneer an imaginative and innovative general education curriculum, especially in such a large urban university, meant that there was little in the experience of similar campuses from which to borrow. For these and other reasons the curriculum was not nurtured with the care it needed. Rather, it was approved and let go, with only a small, weak committee to sustain it. As the community dissolved, so did the curriculum.

BOX 5–2 *(Continued)*

The College of Arts and Sciences has recently begun to reform its general education curriculum. The college is currently developing courses to meet the new language, mathematics, and science requirements mandated by eight university-wide general education goals, which were established in 1993. In addition, a new model, first proposed in 1991, has several notable features, including a series of interdisciplinary collegiate seminars. Students are required to take three seminars, each focusing on a theme and on several critical-thinking skills.

who came to feel confident and excited about it in the classroom— was too small to sustain it in the face of those who were indifferent or who would disown it altogether. Departmental boundaries at the university for the most part remained impermeable to general education: Faculty remained loyal largely to their departments and disciplines, so that recruiting faculty to teach in the new program became a matter of arm-twisting.

Further eroding the enthusiasm for the curriculum were severe budget cuts, faculty and staff layoffs, and program reductions—all contributing to the formation of a defensive if not paranoid climate. A highly centralized state higher education bureaucracy gave many faculty and administrators the sense that the locus of control was far removed from their work lives. As a result, administrators came to behave more like middle managers rather than leaders, and mutual scapegoating between administrators and faculty increased.[4] As one faculty member described the situation: "Faculty have withdrawn from the Core [as the program was known] and the university in general because they are tired and depressed, worn down by the endless assault on the quality of life in this university."

In contrast, the work of the general education committees at the University of Minnesota, Morris was woven into
the fabric of institutional life (see Box 5–3). This was not due

---

BOX 5–3   Close-up: University of Minnesota, Morris

In the farmland of west central Minnesota, some three
hours' drive from Minneapolis, is the town of Morris,
population 5,600—approximately half the size of the
undergraduate student body at the University of Massachusetts Boston. Like the University of Massachusetts Boston, the University of Minnesota, Morris came
into being during the expansionist 1960s. As described
in the university's bulletin and heard repeatedly in interviews, since its inception it has prided itself on providing individual attention and challenging, small undergraduate classes for an academically talented, handpicked student body. In 1991, 40 percent of all fresh-
men were in the top 5 percent of their high school
classes, and 82 percent were in the top 20 percent; 44
percent of students' fathers had bachelor's degrees.
Morris enrolls approximately 1,900 students. The campus is neither local nor regional, but a state institution, a rural, residential alternative to the large, urban flagship campus. In 1991, only 6 percent of the students lived within 25 miles of Morris; 32 percent came
from the Twin Cities area, and the rest from around
the state.

The University of Minnesota, Morris faculty in the
early 1980s had become dissatisfied with the looseness of
the general education program and had obtained external funds (Title III) to revise it. In the early 1980s the
Minnesota state legislature and the governor began look-

BOX 5–3 *(Continued)*

faculty member, "a source of savings." Enrollments at Morris had declined in the late 1970s but were rebounding.

In 1981, in a real jolt to the campus, the school's budget was cut for the first time in its history. Echoing the thoughts of several others, a faculty leader stated, "We were threatened with closing [at that time], but these were very subtle threats. The question for us was how to avoid being just another [University of Minnesota] campus. We needed to be distinctive in order to save ourselves."

The head of the University of Minnesota had made clear to each campus what he thought its strengths were and, by implication, what it ought to emphasize. In Morris's case he conveyed that the institution should take on a distinctive identity as a quality liberal arts college in the University of Minnesota system. In large part this was consistent with Morris's existing undergraduate mission, although there had once been talk of increasing the number of master's programs on campus. The plan to reinvigorate the liberal arts seemed increasingly like a directive, one for which the contours were familiar and valued and one that virtually everyone accepted in principle.

No additions have been made to the general education curriculum since the time of the campus visit. In 1991/92 a General Education Assessment Committee recommended both simplification of the general education requirements and possible elimination of the freshman core course. Two subsequent committees have struggled to design an acceptable core course, without much success. The issue is now on hold because the larger university is moving to the semester system. In addition, because of severe budget cuts the freshman core course, Inquiry, will not be offered after 1995. Nonetheless, the Campus Assembly recently voted to support the continuation of a core course requirement.

to the greater perspicacity of individual actors, although talented individuals made a difference; rather, it was attributable to an already existing sense of community and mutuality that, while not markedly strong, sufficed to weaken the constraints imposed on individual action by the university bureaucracy.

At Morris the newness of the school and its singular, unchanged mission, recently reinforced at the urging of the system's president, meant that the central question was not whether to develop vigorous, innovative general education but rather what form it should take. In this sense, faculty were on the same page from the outset. Still, the campus was cleaved, with the major division being between the primarily older founding faculty in the humanities division and the mid-career and more liberal faculty in the division of social sciences who, chafing under the domination of the old guard, wanted to make their mark in the university. Almost everyone interviewed made unprompted reference to these coalitions. On the surface the conflict was over resource allocation (specifically, 12 new faculty positions that would help carry the teaching burden of the new program) and political and educational orthodoxy. Beneath the surface, however, was a subtext: With general education as the vehicle, a cohort of mid-career faculty, hired as the second generation of the University of Minnesota, Morris's teaching staff, was attempting to gain political and cultural ascendancy. Said one observer: "Some [Humanities faculty] felt that they were changing the ball game and that they wouldn't be as powerful as they were once." Said another:

> Humanities faculty feel they are no longer playing an important role in the life of the college and that they have been separated from the main line the institution has taken. . . . They have been disenfranchised and this is being played out through the general education program to an extent. . . . They didn't approve the program and now with heavy general education teaching responsibilities they have the feeling of being [set] upon.

The campus was at odds. At the risk of oversimplification, the group attempting to wrest control was akin to a young adult who, in his attempt to individuate and carve out some autonomy from the stodgy older folks, rules out their solutions not because they do not work but because they are not his own.

Still, at a small place like the University of Minnesota, Morris it was easy to bring most people together at one time so that general education proposals could be fully debated. In addition, much was done on the campus to create support for the program. In particular, faculty development efforts were frequent and, for the most part, useful. These included summer retreats that focused on how to teach the freshman core course. The source of the program's strength and vitality was the majority of faculty who believed the program was intellectually engaging for students because that was their own shared experience of it. Unlike the situation at the University of Massachusetts Boston, the nucleus of supporters was sufficiently large to ensure the curriculum's survival through its early years.

At Seattle University the sense of community, informed by Jesuit tradition, was even stronger than that at the University of Minnesota, Morris. Interestingly, most undergraduate faculty were not Jesuits, and fewer than half were Catholic. Younger, urbane, discipline-oriented faculty still found attractive the Jesuit emphasis on the uses of learning for the betterment of society and the "recognition that God intends them to be responsible as a community" (Donahue, 1990, p. 54). The faculty were decidedly uninterested in remaking the university in the image of a generic all-purpose university; whether religious or lay, faculty found in the Jesuit philosophy a source of coherence and character for the curriculum.

The process of designing, approving, and implementing the new program was not uniformly smooth and frictionless. Antagonisms surfaced, setbacks occurred, and progress was slow, halting, and erratic. Yet three features distinguished the change process at Seattle University. First, despite questions of resource allocation and legitimacy, the debate at Seattle was framed not in terms of winners and losers but in terms of how values could be incorporated into a renewed vision for the university. Second, despite faculty complaints that the university administration in general had an authoritarian top-down style, administrators remained on the sidelines throughout the debates. Although the deans and the provost appointed members of the design committee—a critical power—they then stepped back, limiting their role to that of observers. No one could recall an incident during the design phase in which university officials intruded or unduly influenced the proceedings.

Most critically, faculty and administration at Seattle University had an appreciation of their actual dependence on each other for creating and sustaining the conditions that would allow them to achieve the goals of the curriculum, whether educational or organizational. Such maturity, a central ingredient of community, is consistent with the repeated findings in sociological research that interest in innovation increases as people feel more secure, especially if that security is based on competence (Gross & Etzioni, 1985).

Third, for faculty at Seattle University as well as at the University of Minnesota, Morris and several of the other institutions, the seminar-like quality of the curriculum design process was crucial to the success of general education. Sessions on the nature of the university in a modern society, new ways of organizing and conveying knowledge, the nature and boundaries of knowledge, and the modeling of proposed interdisciplinary or capstone courses generated an authentic excitement. Faculty recounted these days as heady and during interviews recreated an almost palpable enthusiasm. The strong consensus was that these activities were "wonderful and exciting . . . people were willing to speak frankly and listen without defensiveness. There was lots of compromising and politicking. It was the building of a sense of community that had never been as high."

Similarly, on the more successful campuses, faculty reported a renewed interest in teaching, more communication between departments and faculty, and an intellectual enrichment through strong faculty-development programs that continued beyond the date of the new program's implementation. These planning sessions were, in effect, a further general education of, by, and for the faculty.

IDEALIZED VISIONS OF GENERAL EDUCATION

A second tenet of ideal culture, especially among arts and sciences faculty, was that the curriculum should not be adulterated by real-world, short-run concerns, that it should instead be born of educational motives pure and crystalline, *lux et veritas*. Idealized and even utopian visions for general education were typically presented in the early stages of a design committee's deliberations. From a sociological perspective, such declarations of purpose and commitment played a vital role: They helped celebrate and reaffirm cherished values regarding the "goodness" of higher learning and thereby enhanced a sense of guild specialness and solidarity. Such pronouncements were, in effect, reminders that the professoriate was an important agency, although not the only one, in defining and framing matters of fundamental importance to all: the nature of nature, of human nature, of society's and people's relation to nature, and, in schools of theology, even the nature of supernature. Like academic regalia, these formalized discussions of the good and the true were boundary-maintaining devices that helped uphold the professoriate as a distinctive group and the campus as a unique social institution.

Unanimity regarding the curriculum was never reached nor was it even necessary; paradoxically, a sense of professional membership—and mutual enjoyment—often obtained in forums where faculty irritated one another in some socially prescribed, ritualistic manner.

Early talk of general education reform spread quickly through each institution, with considerations, especially by practical-minded administrators, of how it might solve a host of institutional problems. A new general education program, it was thought, might help reverse declining student enrollment; shore up the student body's academic deficiencies; attract donors to the campus; assist in the consolidation of programs or campuses mandated by a state authority, as in the case of the University of Massachusetts Boston; thwart a threatened loss of accreditation; bolster a sagging college reputation; or spread students around to various academic departments so that faculty jobs would not be lost (the "garbage-can" model mentioned in the previous chapter).

Subtexts were also part of a campus's real culture but were tied less to issues of administrative practicality and more to those of ideological, intellectual, and political substance. Some were obvious, such as the extent to which feminism would find expression in the curriculum; others formed a backdrop, as when general education at Morris served as the vehicle through which the cohort of mid-career faculty attempted to put its mark on the campus. A chronic strain was present from the beginning of a campus's deliberations. The ideal vision for general education did not take into account real-world institutional problems. Indeed, idealism often clashed with the more practical elements of a campus's mission, such as the provision of vocational or preprofessional education. Such education was not always looked down upon. Rather, the designers—at least those from arts and sciences departments—were dismayed at having to diminish their vision to satisfy the demands for credit hours by the professional school's accrediting associations. In summary, although the designers initially looked toward some larger intellectual vision, the remainder of the design process was typically one of compromise; attenuation; and, from their perspective, disappointment.

The contradictions between the ideal and the real eventually became evident. The glittering campus rhetoric bumped up against bleak institutional realities—budget limitations, the academic deficiencies of a student body, the unwillingness or inability of many faculty to teach general education courses, and many other institutional problems. The question then became, "What is the most we can do, given our present situation and our present circumstances?" In this way what began as an attempt to institutionalize utopian ideals through the curriculum became little more than the calibration of academic life with organizational necessity. In short, *educational* goals receded into the background as campuses became more concerned with how a new program could meet other *organizational* goals.

If it is community that a campus wants, instituting general education is not a direct route to it. Indeed, on campuses where reform efforts sputtered, some professors were deeply wounded. They had invested heavily in a new curriculum, only to see their hopes contract into a program that no one wanted but most would accept.

Students, too, react to general education. Although students usually believe in some abstraction called "education," in some colleges those who study too hard and learn too much risk being considered traitors by their classmates.[5] The mores of some student cultures proscribe excessive academic achievement. This may be the case with general education, often seen as something to "get through." On one campus, students renamed the required first-year course from "Ways of Knowing" to "Waste of Knowing." To what extent, then, can a curriculum help create a community of learners that permits students to work at a level higher than they initially bargained for?

General education reform does not, by itself, create community. However, it can be defeated by the absence of or enhanced by the presence of community. Campuses with a feeling of mutuality deal more effectively with innovation than do fragmented campuses that, by extension, require some sense of community before a coherent curricular experiment can be undertaken.

NOTES

1. This conception of community was inspired by Robert Edwards, president of Bowdoin College.

2. For a full discussion of community, see the Carnegie Foundation for the Advancement of Teaching, *Campus Life: In Search of Community* (1990).

3. For an account of community in Puritan New England see Perry Miller, *Errand Into the Wilderness* (1956).

4. Paraphrased from Robert Birnbaum, *How Colleges Work* (1988), p. 16.

5. The authors are indebted to Everett Hughes for this insight.

▶ 6

From Struggle to Reform

Four years ago, it was not uncommon to have seniors in class who had never read a novel.
—FACULTY MEMBER, ROGER WILLIAMS COLLEGE

Every college and university requires undergraduates to take general education courses. Except for the teaching of writing skills, however, little agreement exists about the subject content and other skills that should be the core of the general education curriculum. Western civilization, multiculturalism, internationalism, interdisciplinary education, civics, and the Great Books all have their advocates. Even in colleges and universities that have forged a consensus about the content of their general education programs, faculty and administrators complain about the quality of student learning in the liberal arts.

There is enough blame to go around. Some critics think that weaknesses in general education stem from faculty indifference to undergraduate teaching. Others hold that problems are created by ideological faculty from the left and the right who control the curriculum. Asked why general education is so problematic, younger faculty members will say it is because of its poor philosophical basis. How can students learn to think well and to understand the great ideas in several disciplines if the conceptual basis for the program is flawed? Whatever possessed you, they will ask their senior colleagues, to make so many compromises? Senior colleagues, who may have participated in previous efforts to reform general education, are more forgiving. They will reply that changing general education is one of the most difficult efforts a campus can undertake. What other activity, they will ask, requires that almost everyone on a campus—the dean, the professor of history, and the professor of accounting—agree on a common set of principles? What else has as much significance for faculty workloads and departmental lines, for how students spend their time, and for how records are kept? If there is fault to be allocated, faculty are likely to blame administrators and boards of trustees for not supporting general education adequately while at the same time calling for reform. In turn, administrators and trustees might attribute weaknesses in the curriculum to the culture of the academy, which gives faculty too much power and freedom.

While college and university people have been preoccupied with these questions, the outside world—especially state legislatures, higher education organizations, and regional accrediting agencies—has seen the poor quality of general education as a symbol of all that is wrong with the academy. To those outside higher education, general education is the litmus test for educational quality. If college graduates cannot think clearly, cannot write decent prose, and cannot analyze and debate, how effective can the general education curriculum be? A college degree, by the very arguments put forth by higher education leaders, should be the guarantor of an educated person.

THE CONTEXT OF REFORM: COLLEGES AND UNIVERSITIES IN A TIME OF SCARCITY

These criticisms come at a time when higher education is facing budget cuts and challenges to its legitimacy. The kinds of colleges and universities in this study have been dependent for most of their budgets on student tuition or public funds. Buffeted by economic, political, and demographic misfortune before the rest of higher education was, they have survived reorganizations, mergers, and threats of closure. Many began as one type of institution—a normal school, a technical institute, a church-related college—and evolved into something else. Their faculty have struggled for years to reconcile their ideal of being faculty members with the actuality of their working lives, which includes economic insecurity, heavy teaching loads, limited resources for scholarship, and decrepit classrooms. The colleges and universities discussed in previous chapters have much to teach other institutions about maintaining commitment to the ideals of general education in the face of adversity. Nowhere has the struggle to revitalize general education been greater. Faculty on these campuses have spent hours in committee meetings, poring over proposals for change, negotiating the details of curriculum change with colleagues from different disciplines. Senior administrators have prodded and cajoled faculty, shifted resources, and met the demands of accrediting bodies to improve general education. Registrars have worked overtime to develop new schedules and systems of credit counting as they tried to keep up with the changes wrought by faculty and administration.

This book has turned the critical discussion of general education on its side. Through detailed observation it has discovered how campuses, actually navigate the waters of change in higher education, especially in a time of scarcity. As faculty members and administrators themselves, the authors wanted to show critics and supporters alike that general education could be both improved and revitalized. At the same time the book provides ample evidence that changing general education is rarely an unadulterated success. A perfect process exists only on paper.

TEXTS AND SUBTEXTS

Theories abound about how decisions should be made in the corporate and nonprofit sectors of the economy. Common to almost all is a belief in the efficacy of rational argument and collective goal setting. Rational decision making is valued especially in colleges and universities, where faculty are esteemed for their ability to present well-reasoned arguments. When considering changes in the curriculum, faculty are expected to debate, judiciously and objectively, the merits of carefully designed educational models. The language of debate about general education—couched in abstract discussions of what students should know—itself lends credence to the view that the process of curriculum change is a rational one. As demonstrated throughout this book, the reality is much more complicated. Changing general education requires give-and-take among many actors and units with different interests, cultures, and needs. Throughout the change process, and especially at the beginning when a new curriculum is being designed, conflict may be inevitable and even desirable as a way of bringing out and adjudicating these differences before they undermine the final outcome.

In this change process three powerful influences, or subtexts, are shaping both conflicts and their resolutions. The need for economic security, the most important of the three, is followed by the competition for legitimacy and resources and by the desire for community. The need for economic security causes faculty members to define issues narrowly: How will change affect me and my closest colleagues? Because economic security cannot be taken for granted, especially in tuition-dependent institutions, its absence can be a powerful determinant of decisions about general education. Many faculty members fear that they are unemployable outside of academia; the cumulative effect of crises in their institutions, attacks on tenure, and layoffs in other industries intensifies their fears.

The competition for legitimacy and resources plays out against economic insecurity but operates as a distinct subtext. Although general education has certain undesirable aspects from the faculty's point of view, especially in taking their attention away from their departments and their research, it can endow units and individuals, particularly those in the liberal arts, with valuable status. As students have increasingly preferred vocational preparation over the liberal arts and as institutions responded by shifting resources from the liberal arts to professional programs, liberal arts faculty have been left with few means of maintaining or regaining their legitimacy. The inclusion of a subject as a requirement in the general education curriculum is one of those means. It is also a symbol of the importance of certain fields to the mission and standing of their institutions. There are also positive resource implications of such decisions. Because required courses must be taught frequently, additional faculty are often hired to supplement the teaching activities of current faculty.

The desire for community is the third powerful subtext. The culture of collaboration has recently given way to centralized decision making as administrators strive to keep their campuses financially solvent and independent in the face of declining resources, increased competition for students, and pressures from regional and state education forces determined to become major players in the higher education arena. As the campus has become more fractionalized, faculty and administrators have begun to yearn for the past, when campus life was more tranquil and communal. Even if they have not actually experienced such a life, it is an ideal that brought them to college teaching or administration.

THE SEARCH FOR SOLUTIONS

The desire for meaningful work motivates faculty as much as it does other human beings. Contrary to what is sometimes reported in the media and elsewhere, most college and university faculty are devoted to teaching. They care deeply about their students' education and, as a consequence, have strong and passionate views of what students should learn in college. As a group, indeed, they are often the harshest critics of their own campuses' general education programs. Fearing that change will bring turmoil, conflict, and economic insecurity, they cling to what they know and what they have done in the past. This book pays close attention to these fears, for they greatly influence the reform of general education. Even the most ardent faculty critics of the status quo have been reluctant to set the general education change process in motion. Those who are interested are often overwhelmed by the prospect of organizing such a comprehensive effort. On most campuses, participation in research, departmental service, and teaching is more highly valued than participation in college- or university-wide teaching programs.

However, chief academic administrators have been less reluctant. Pressures from the outside coupled with dissatisfaction (their own and the faculty's) with current educational practices have motivated them to take the first steps toward reform. The process usually begins with the appointment of an ad hoc group charged with recommending a new or improved general education program. Questions are raised. What do graduates need to know to be gainfully employed and responsible citizens? What common learning is important? What skills are critical?

Implicit in these questions is the understanding that some educational values are sacrosanct. Broadly accepted by faculty and administrators alike, these values provide justification for the decision to begin the curriculum change process.

For example, many campuses view strengthening students' writing and thinking abilities as a sine qua non of any self-respecting college. Others choose as reason for reform the teaching of a particular content, such as multiculturalism or internationalism, or a particular curricular structure—more requirements, fewer choices, greater coherence.

Coalitions are formed to increase the chances that change will go a certain way. Liberal arts faculty view general education reform as a way to regain the prestige and resources lost over the last several decades to faculty in professional fields. Younger faculty treat general education reform as an arena in which to wrest power from the older generation. Departments push for autonomy, while community-minded faculty see general education as a vehicle for building colleagueship beyond departments or divisions.

The process of general education change is characteristically a search for consensus among groups and individuals. No text or subtext is exempt from negotiation. The power to influence outcomes depends upon both formal and informal authority. Authority is derived from formal positions in the university bureaucracy or in the change process. The chair of a governance committee, a member of a curriculum design committee, or a dean all have formal authority. Informal authority is a function of the legitimacy and prestige accorded individuals and units. Senior faculty have more informal authority than do junior faculty; well-respected teachers have more informal authority than do those with poor teaching reputations; prolific scholars have more informal authority than do faculty with limited publishing records; groups of faculty have more informal power than do individual faculty. The search for a consensus is concluded when a solution addresses both the texts, the educational goals of change, and the subtexts of those groups or individuals who, by their formal or informal authority, have the most influence over the outcome of the process.

THE SHAPE OF REFORM

Is general education reform worth the effort? Formal assessments of change would provide a partial answer. However, although many of the campuses in this study intended to evaluate the impact of their reform efforts, few have actually done so.

To answer the question, this book has reported on the views of the people who knew best, participants in the struggle for reform. Telephone interviews with 71 of them, primarily administrators, revealed that general education reform has produced more structured programs than the loose programs of the 1970s. For the most part, institutions have tightened the distribution system—requiring students to take more courses or certain types of courses, such as interdisciplinary or critical-thinking courses. In the absence of hard data or a systematic review, participants were reluctant to make judgments about the impact of the new programs on student learning. For the most part, faculty believed that efforts to improve critical-thinking skills have resulted in better prepared students and that limits on the choice of courses have produced a more coherent education. Liberal arts faculty, especially, have welcomed the limits on student choice. Under the previous system permitting wide-ranging choices the students' vocational interests led them to bypass many liberal arts offerings in favor of general education courses that were closely linked to their majors and that had practical value.

Those interviewed on campus visits, most of whom were faculty, had more to say about the impact of general education changes on faculty than on students. Faculty most engaged in the change process depicted their experiences as energizing. They became more aware of the relationship between their courses and the institution's educational goals. They cited positive impacts on their teaching skills. They were especially grateful for the opportunity to work with faculty members from other departments or schools. Many mentioned that participating in the general education reform had renewed their sense of being part of an intellectual community.

Reform efforts also produced disappointment. The most common reaction was that educational change was too modest. Participants in design committees, who developed the conceptual framework for the curriculum, were often disappointed in the final outcomes of their efforts. They had put energy and time into creating a conceptually strong program, only to see it subjected to criticism and compromise. Many viewed the search for consensus as a sign of weakness. A few, especially those deeply engaged from the beginning, vowed never again to take part in reforming general education.

A common negative effect of the change process was the exacerbation of tensions between faculty and administrators. Faculty, especially those on campuses with much economic insecurity, read any administrative interest in changing general education as an attempt to control their deliberations and as frontal attacks on the faculty's already shaky power and authority.

TOWARD BETTER IMPLEMENTATION

The book has shown that a curriculum change process that is open and collaborative is the only way to ensure that faculty will feel committed to the eventual outcome. An open and collaborative process, however, is also likely to result in compromise and the dilution of the original reform goals. As discussed, faculty members and administrators believe in rational decision making. They argue that an effective change process is, by definition, one that produces the intended goals. Anything less, especially if it results in questionable compromises, is a disappointment. In the current culture of colleges and universities, however, educational outcomes cannot be separated from organizational processes. Administrators cannot carry out general education programs by themselves; they need faculty to teach in them and to do so effectively. Educationally sound programs depend on the energies and talents of faculty, willingly given, to bring them to life. One result of an open and collaborative change process is that it builds trust and goodwill. Goodwill has a ripple effect, motivating faculty to teach courses in general education and encouraging administrators and staff to support its implementation adequately.

Academic leaders need not be visionaries or charismatic figures to have major impacts on their institutions. Wise leaders on campuses know that they have to remain in the background after appointing a committee to deal with general education. They may keep track of what the committee does, but they cannot do this too often or too openly. Indeed, effective leadership in general education often requires that senior administrators get behind rather than in front of people, guiding them along a path of deliberation that leads to achievable improvements. Those improvements are not necessarily bold and new but incremental. In a crisis, leaders sometimes undertake daring efforts to save an institution. The payoffs of such tactics are high. So, too, are the risks. Unless institutional survival is at stake, it is a mistake for administrators to lead the effort to reform general education. Such strategies can engender deep and lasting discord in the college community, making it difficult for faculty to work with one another and with administrators on general education or other issues.

The best way to achieve significant reform in general education is to view change not as a one-time event but as a continuing effort in which each iteration deepens different aspects of the reform. Campuses that were successful in reforming their general education programs exhibited certain common characteristics. They expected conflict and were willing to compromise, encouraged an open design process, prepared for implementation, recruited qualified teachers, provided professional development activities, offered rewards and incentives to faculty, provided predictable and sufficient resources, and prepared for program evaluation.

1. *Conflict and compromise.* Given the still relatively decentralized structure of colleges and universities, faculty independence, and the loose coupling among departments and between departments and administration, conflict is a predictable aspect of academic life. Efforts to change general education concern the whole institution and inevitably entail disagreement about the content, structure, and philosophy of what should be done. Those who bring about successful change accept and even welcome conflict and look for ways to negotiate differences.

2. *Open design process.* Because faculty have a good deal of autonomy in how they spend their time, successful general education reform depends ultimately upon an institution's ability to attract faculty to teach in the program. Faculty should be encouraged to participate in the design of the new curriculum. This is likely to excite them about working in the program and helping to realize the program's potential. Administrators do well to maintain contact with those engaged in planning the new curriculum but should not themselves take part in it.

3. *Preparation for implementation.* Coming up with a design is only the first step in change. The real work of general education reform takes place after a proposal has been accepted, when deciding on the details and making resources available are crucial. Successful programs are coordinated, protected, nurtured, and monitored. Here administrators can make or break a new general education program, as only they control organization-wide resources. They must provide sufficient resources for the program as well as appoint a well-respected administrator (often a faculty member on release time from teaching) to attend to the concrete tasks of implementing the program.

4. *Recruitment of qualified teachers.* Faculty representing different disciplines and new areas, including interdisciplinary subjects and instruction in skills such as writing and critical thinking, may be called for in a new general education curriculum. Successful programs recruit current or new faculty to teach in them. They avoid drafting unwilling or poorly prepared teachers to satisfy a department's need to staff certain general education courses.

5. *Professional development activities.* Current and future faculty must understand and support the goals of a new program; therefore, faculty-development activities carried out before the program's implementation are critical, especially for course construction. Professional development activities include workshops, retreats, release time to master new materials and pedagogies, collaborative course development, and ongoing faculty seminars. Experienced administrators know that these efforts need not be expensive. Judicious, strategic use of release time and well-planned faculty seminars and special events are not necessarily costly and are especially valuable in supporting faculty preparation for teaching general education courses.

6. *Rewards and incentives.* When considering whether to become a member of a general education committee or to volunteer to teach a general education course, faculty want to know how involvement will affect them. This is a critical issue. The period of early implementation, when campuses depend upon faculty of goodwill to staff the program, is an especially fragile time for general education reform. Faculty who participate in general education reform need to be encouraged and rewarded. Teaching in general education courses should be evaluated and considered in tenure and promotion decisions.

7. *Predictable and sufficient resources.* Grants sometimes carry a new curriculum through its initial years. Symbolic, one-time only resources given to the general education program by presidents, deans, and provosts are also important because they foster a climate of belief in the program. Nevertheless, long-term funding should be a priority built into the implementation of general education programs. Because senior administrators seldom remain in their institutions as long as faculty do, those who support reform must see to it that predictable resources to sustain the program are built in early. These resources need not be extravagant, but they must be sufficient.

8. *Program evaluation.* A thorough evaluation of the changes should begin at implementation, before problems become insoluble and errors become institutionalized. Evaluation should be seen as part of an ongoing process of assessment and reform of general education.

These characteristics of successful reform indicate that even in difficult circumstances it is possible to improve general education. The details of the process not only determine success but also carry a much larger meaning. In many respects, general education curricula are sociological Rorschachs for American higher education. Americans project onto them their collective anxieties and aspirations regarding the academy, the next generation, and even civilization itself. General education curricula provide powerful data as cultural artifacts and, as such, they should be treated no differently and no less dispassionately than any other artifact. This has been the chief aim of this book.

The very process of designing, approving, and implementing general education programs—carrying as it does so much symbolic, organizational, and personal meaning—inevitably engages most academic divisions and departments. So central is general education to a campus's identity that an institution's approach to changing it tells much about its past, present, and immediate future as well as its weaknesses and strengths. In the end the process of reforming general education in a period of scarcity and uncertainty reveals a campus's capacity to act as a responsible community, to make necessary educational change even as it tends to the needs of its members.

► APPENDIX A

Methodology

The goal of this study was to document the process of general education curriculum reform. The following research questions served as underpinnings for the research.

From a Data Collection Standpoint . . .

1. What are the common characteristics of a design process, and what factors are associated with more successful change?
2. What are the common implementation issues, and what factors are associated with more successful implementation?

From an Analytical Standpoint . . .

1. How do sociological, organizational, and political paradigms help us understand the process of general education reform?
2. How can these data and analyses inform future reform efforts?

The researchers identified the population of interest as New England colleges and universities with limited resources (see Introduction concerning the selection of this sector) and decided on a two-stage design of data collection. The first stage was a telephone survey to gain a broad perspective of when and how general education reform took place on these campuses. Additionally the researchers wanted to know the extent of change in their general education programs. The plan was to conduct in-depth studies of campuses identified as having experienced major change in their programs. These campuses, it was thought, would exhibit in bold relief the elemental practices that contribute to successful change. However, although many had attempted it, only a few campuses had accomplished major change; most had realized only minor or moderate change. This finding led to the addition of another research question:

3. What factors are associated with the magnitude of curricular change; i.e., what distinguishes those institutions that accomplished major change from those that accomplished more modest change?

The telephone survey data were also used to identify campuses for in-depth qualitative case studies. The two research methods, the telephone study and the campus visits, are described in greater detail below.

TELEPHONE SURVEY

A telephone survey of 71 New England colleges and universities was conducted in spring through fall 1989. The campuses were primarily those defined by the Carnegie Foundation for the Advancement of Teaching (1994) as "master's colleges and universities" and "baccalaureate colleges II." (These terms were adopted in 1994; the earlier term for master's institutions was "comprehensive" institutions, and the earlier term for baccalaureate colleges was "liberal arts colleges.") A few doctoral universities II that resembled master's institutions and one research university were included.

Master's I institutions were defined as those institutions offering a full range of baccalaureate degrees and graduate education through the master's degree and awarding 40 or more master's degrees annually in three or more disciplines; master's II institutions award 20 or more master's degrees annually in one or more disciplines. Baccalaureate II institutions are primarily undergraduate colleges that emphasize baccalaureate degree programs, are less selective in admissions policies than baccalaureate I colleges, and typically award less than 40 percent of their degrees in liberal arts fields (whereas baccalaureate I institutions are restrictive in admissions and award 40 percent or more of their degrees in the liberal arts).

The Carnegie Foundation identified the other major categories of institutions as follows: research universities I, which annually receive at least $40 million in federal support and annually award at least 50 doctoral degrees, and research universities II, which annually receive between $15.5 million and $40 million in federal support and annually award at least 50 doctoral degrees; doctoral universities I, which annually award at least 40 doctoral degrees in five or more disciplines, and doctoral universities II, which annually award at least 10 doctoral degrees in at least three disciplines or at least 20 in one or more disciplines; baccalaureate (liberal arts colleges) I, which award at least 40 percent of their baccalaureate degrees in the liberal arts and are restrictive in admissions; associate of arts colleges, which offer associate of arts certificate or degree programs; and specialized institutions. (The definitions of these classifications are reprinted here by permission from the Carnegie Foundation for the Advancement of Teaching.)

The 71 institutions selected for the telephone survey (see Appendix B) included 26 that offered advanced degrees in addition to the bachelor's and 49 that offered associate's degrees in addition to the bachelor's. Two thirds (47) of these institutions were private, and one third (24) was public.

The researchers developed an extensive protocol (see Appendix C) to gather information on general institutional characteristics, current and former general education requirements, and elements of the change process: reasons for change, committee composition, length of process, use of additional resources, dynamics of decision making, and implementation issues. Over an 18-month period from 1989 to 1991 trained NERCHE researchers conducted telephone interviews with campus officers familiar with general education. On most of the campuses the senior academic officer (a provost, dean, or vice-president) was interviewed, although occasionally a researcher was directed to the president, a faculty member, or another individual who was knowledgeable about this topic. In some cases more than one person on a campus was interviewed.

Quantitative survey data were coded and analyzed using the Statistical Analysis System (SAS). Open-ended comments were read and summarized by several readers to get a flavor of the major issues facing the campuses in conducting curriculum change. These data informed the selection of campuses for the in-depth study as well as the development of the protocol for campus visits. An important feature of the data analysis entailed evaluating each campus's present and former general education curriculum according to the following categories:

- Distribution system: a choice of courses
- Modified distribution system: mostly a choice of courses, with some required courses
- Modified core: mostly required courses, with some choice
- Core: all required courses

After categorizing present and former programs and reviewing the comments of the campus spokesperson, the researchers were able to quantify the amount of change that had occurred in the most recent curriculum redesign. At this point they discovered that only nine campuses in the sample had experienced major change, precipitating the addition of the new research question to examine factors associated with the extent of change.

CAMPUS VISITS

Several criteria were used to select institutions for intensive case study. First, because the researchers discovered that few institutions had implemented substantial change, they abandoned the plan of examining only institutions that had experienced such change. They decided instead to visit a range of institutions—those that had achieved minimal, moderate, or substantial reforms—to better understand the relationship between institutional situations and the magnitude of change. Second, the researchers wanted to examine programs that had been in place for several years so that the history of the program's implementation could be analyzed. Third, they wanted to include a range of institutions geographically distributed throughout the region, both publicly and privately financed, with a variety of missions and of different sizes. The following 12 institutions were selected for campus visits from among the participants in the telephone survey:

> Albertus Magnus College, New Haven, Connecticut
> Bridgewater State College, Bridgewater, Massachusetts
> Colby-Sawyer College, New London, New Hampshire
> Green Mountain College, Poultney, Vermont
> Johnson State College, Johnson, Vermont
> New England College, Henniker, New Hampshire
> Plymouth State College, Plymouth, New Hampshire
> Roger Williams College, Bristol, Rhode Island
> University of Bridgeport, Bridgeport, Connecticut
> University of Hartford, West Hartford, Connecticut
> University of Maine at Machias, Machias, Maine
> University of Massachusetts Boston, Boston,
>   Massachusetts

The researchers also wished to broaden the geographical scope of the study to test their findings in institutions outside New England. After consulting with a total of eight higher education researchers, consultants, and other experts in the field, the researchers reviewed catalogues from 26 recommended institutions and conducted a telephone survey with chief academic officers or their designees at each campus. On the basis of the campuses' geographic location, their diverse status (both public and private, master's and baccalaureate), and evidence that significant changes had been made in their general education curriculum, the team selected three institutions for in-depth analysis:

Kean College, Union, New Jersey
Seattle University, Seattle, Washington
University of Minnesota, Morris, Morris, Minnesota

The final sample thus included 15 institutions for intensive case studies.

Guided by the research questions and the results of the telephone survey, the researchers developed an extensive protocol of 113 questions (see Appendix D). Questions probed the background of respondents, their career paths and their past and present involvement in the general education program; the impetus for change in the general education curriculum; the timetable of the change process; elements of the change process (committee composition and responsibility, activities of the committee, identification of all parties involved in the process, etc.); points of agreement and opposition; persons who supported and opposed change; channels of campus governance involved; faculty and administrative leadership; and details of implementation.

During 1991 and 1992, teams of two or three researchers visited the 15 campuses. The two-day visits consisted of interviews with administrators, faculty, and staff identified as active in the planning or implementation of the new general education program. Opponents as well as proponents, program implementors, witnesses, and historians were interviewed in sessions lasting from 60 to 90 minutes. On some campuses, students were asked for their impressions of the current program. On every campus, everyone with whom the teams met was extraordinarily cordial, providing materials and all manner of access for this research.

During these visits the researchers took extensive notes, sometimes tape recording interviews, and gathered as many historical materials, such as meeting minutes, as possible. Upon returning from the campus visit, each team member transcribed field notes and added summary comments. The chairperson of each visiting team, working from team members' transcribed interviews and drawing upon the materials gathered, wrote a full-length case document describing both the history and the mission of the campus as well as the details of the most recent general education reform. In this way 15 complete cases were compiled for further analysis by the team.

After all cases were complete, the complex task of analyzing the data began. The researchers met monthly over the course of a year to note similarities and contradictions in the case materials, identify important themes, and develop a structure for presenting the material. In this way the project evolved to the present analytic structure, which focuses on the organizational, political, and cultural aspects of the change process.

In 1995, the project director called each of the 15 institutions' senior academic officer to learn whether the institution had modified or had plans to modify its general education programs. Seven institutions were then reviewing general education yet again, including 3 that were making major changes. Details are provided in the text of the book.

Institutions in the Study

TABLE B–1 Institutions Participating in the Telephone Survey

Institution	Location
Albertus Magnus College[a]	New Haven, Conn.
American International College	Springfield, Mass.
Anna Maria College	Paxton, Mass.
Assumption College	Worcester, Mass.
Atlantic Union College	South Lancaster, Mass.
Boston College	Chestnut Hill, Mass.
Bridgewater State College[a]	Bridgewater, Mass.
Burlington College	Burlington, Vt.
Castleton State College	Castleton, Vt.
Central Connecticut State University	New Britain, Conn.
Clark University	Worcester, Mass.
Colby-Sawyer College[a]	New London, N.H.
College of St. Joseph	Rutland, Vt.
Curry College	Milton, Mass.
Dartmouth College	Hanover, N.H.
Eastern Connecticut State University	Willimantic, Conn.
Emerson College	Boston, Mass.
Fairfield University	Fairfield, Conn.
Fitchburg State College	Fitchburg, Mass.
Framingham State College	Framingham, Mass.
Franklin Pierce College	Rindge, N.H.
Green Mountain College[a]	Poultney, Vt.

(Continued)

TABLE B–1   *(Continued)*

Institution	Location
Hellenic College	Brookline, Mass.
Johnson State College[a]	Johnson, Vt.
Lesley College	Cambridge, Mass.
Merrimac College	North Andover, Mass.
Mount Ida College	Newton Centre, Mass.
New England College[a]	Henniker, N.H.
North Adams State College	North Adams, Mass.
Northeastern University	Boston, Mass.
Norwich University	Northfield, Vt.
Notre Dame College	Manchester, N.H.
Providence College	Providence, R.I.
Quinnipiac College	Hamden, Conn.
Rhode Island College	Providence, R.I.
Rivier College	Nashua, N.H.
Roger Williams College[a]	Bristol, R.I.
Sacred Heart University	Bridgeport, Conn.
Salem State College	Salem, Mass.
Salve Regina—The Newport College	Newport, R.I.
Simmons College	Boston, Mass.
Southeastern Massachusetts University[b]	North Dartmouth, Mass.
Southern Connecticut State University	New Haven, Conn.
Southern Vermont College	Bennington, Vt.
Springfield College	Springfield, Mass.
St. Joseph College	West Hartford, Conn.
St. Joseph's College	North Windham, Maine
St. Michael's College	Winooski, Vt.
Stonehill College	North Easton, Mass.
Suffolk University	Boston, Mass.
Tufts University	Medford, Mass.
Unity College	Unity, Maine
University of Bridgeport[a]	Bridgeport, Conn.
University of Hartford[a]	West Hartford, Conn.
University of Lowell[c]	Lowell, Mass.
University of Maine at Farmington	Farmington, Maine
University of Maine at Machias[a]	Machias, Maine
University of Maine at Orono	Orono, Maine
University of Massachusetts Boston[a]	Boston, Mass.
University of New England	Biddeford, Maine
University of New Hampshire	Durham, N.H.
University of New Haven	West Haven, Conn.
University of Southern Maine	Portland, Maine
University of Vermont	Burlington, Vt.

TABLE B–1 *(Continued)*

Institution	Location
Vermont College	Northfield, Vt.
Westbrook College Portland, Maine	
Western Connecticut State University	Danbury, Conn.
Westfield State College	Westfield, Mass.
Western New England College	Springfield, Mass.
Worcester Polytechnic University	Worcester, Mass.
Worcester State College	Worcester, Mass.

[a]Indicates institution visited for campus visits and case-study analysis. Four additional institutions not shown here—Kean College of New Jersey, Plymouth State College, Seattle University, and the University of Minnesota, Morris—were selected for campus visits.

[b]Now the University of Massachusetts Dartmouth

[c]Now the University of Massachusetts Lowell

TABLE B–2   Profile of Case-Study Institutions

Name	Date of Campus Visit	Status	Type[a]	Degree Offerings[b]	Enroll-ment, 1991[c]
Albertus Magnus College	Feb. 7–8, 1991	Private	Baccalaureate II	Assoc./ Bach.	707
Bridgewater State College	Nov. 21–22, 1991	Public	Masters I	Bach./ Mast.	5,432
Colby-Sawyer College	Nov. 14–15, 1991	Private	Baccalaureate II	Assoc./ Bach.	500
Green Mountain College	Oct. 22–23, 1991	Private	Baccalaureate II	Bach.	620
Johnson State College	Feb. 11–12, 1991	Public	Masters II	Assoc./ Bach./Mast.	1,652
Kean College	Apr. 22–23, 1992	Public	Masters I	Bach./Mast.	12,891
New England College	Apr. 10–11, 1992	Private	Baccalaureate II	Assoc./ Bach./ Mast.	1,171

(Continued)

TABLE B–2   *(Continued)*

Name	Date of Campus Visit	Status	Type[a]	Degree Offerings[b]	Enroll-ment, 1991[c]
Plymouth State College	Apr. 26–27, 1990	Public	Masters I	Assoc./Bach./ Mast.	4,231
Roger Williams College	Mar. 18–19, 1991	Private	Baccalaureate II	Bach.	3,730
Seattle University	May 14–15, 1992	Private	Masters I	Bach./Mast./ Doc.	4,514
University of Bridgeport	Mar. 25–27, 1990	Private	Masters I	Assoc./Bach./ Mast./Doc.	5,258
University of Hartford	Sept. 27–28, 1989	Private	Masters I	Assoc./Bach./ Mast./Doc.	7,528
University of Maine at Machias	Dec. 9–10, 1992	Public	Baccalaureate II	Assoc./Bach.	876
University of Mass-achusetts Boston	May 3–4, 1990	Public	Masters I	Bach./Mast./ Doc.	12,584
University of Minnesota, Morris	May 7–8, 1992	Public	Baccalaureate I	Bach.	2,041

[a]Types are based on the classifications of the Carnegie Foundation for the Advancement of Teaching in *A Classification of Institutions of Higher Education* (1994); see Appendix A for explanation of the classifications.

[b]Degrees (associate's, bachelor's, master's, doctoral) are those offered at the time of the campus visits.

[c]The source for enrollment figures is the *1991 Higher Education Directory* (1991). Washington, DC: Higher Education Publications. Figures combine graduate and undergraduate enrollment.

APPENDIX C

Telephone Survey Questionnaire

New England Resource Center for Higher Education
Project on the Implementation of General Education

Inst. Code: _____

Date:

Institution _____
Address _____
_____

Contact(s)   Name _____
Title _____
Telephone _____
Role _____

Name _____
Title _____
Telephone _____
Role _____

Name _____
Title _____
Telephone _____
Role _____

Code no. _____

NERCHE Interviewer _____

SITE VISIT RECOMMENDATION
(from last page)   1 _____   2 _____   3 _____

Notes:

CURRENT INSTITUTIONAL DATA

1. Enrollment
   - **A.** Total   _____
   - **B.** Full-time   _____
   - **C.** Part-time   _____
   - **D.** Undergrad   _____
   - **E.** Grad   _____
   - **F.** Single-sex—female   _____   (check one)
   - **G.** Single-sex—male   _____
   - **H.** Coeducation   _____

2. Degrees Conferred
   - **A.** Associate's   _____
   - **B.** Bachelor's   _____
   - **C.** Master's   _____

3. Major/Degree Areas
   - **A.** Liberal Arts   _____
   - **B.** Human Services   _____
   - **C.** Business/Management   _____

Code no. _____

D. Education _____
E. Other _____

_____
_____
_____
_____

4. Date Founded _____

5. If major change in college organization/structure, give

Date of change _____
Brief description of change:

CURRENT GENERAL EDUCATION REQUIREMENTS

6. Are there general education requirements?
Y____   N ____

IF NO, NERCHE ASSESSMENT = 0; SKIP to Q 11.
IF YES, CHECK A., B. or C.

A. The same requirements apply to ALL
students _____

IF YES, GO TO QUESTION 9.
B. Requirements differ by major/degree area _____
C. Requirements only apply to some students _____
Describe:

Code no. _____

7. Major/Degree Areas in which general education requirements apply:

   A. Liberal Arts   _____   (check appropriate
   B. Human Services   _____   areas)
   C. Business/Management   _____
   D. Education   _____
   E. Other: _____

   _____

   _____

   _____

   _____

8. Degrees for which general education requirements apply:

   A. ALL   _____
   B. B.A.   _____
   C. B.S.   _____

9. Outline the institution's definition of current general education requirements (if requirements differ by major or
   degree area, describe only those requirements that apply
   to the liberal arts or the B.A. program):

Code no. _____

10. List any other courses required of all students:

_____

11. NERCHE Assessment of current general education requirements:
    0. NONE: No general education requirements _____
    1. DIST: All req. fulfilled by student-chosen courses _____
    2. MOD. DIST: Distribution system with some requirements _____
    3. MOD. CORE: Most prescribed but some free course choice _____
    4. CORE: Every course prescribed: no student choice _____

Code no. _____

START OF INTERVIEW

OLD CURRICULUM

I would like to begin the interview by asking you several questions about the changes that have taken place in your general education requirements.

12. When were the CURRENT general education requirements instituted? _____

13. Were there general education requirements before the current requirements were instituted?   Y ____   N ____

    IF NO, NERCHE ASSESSMENT = 0; SKIP TO Q 19.
    IF YES, CHECK A., B. or C.

    A. The same requirements applied to ALL students. _____

       IF YES, GO TO Q 16.

    B. Requirements differed by major/degree area. _____
    C. Requirements only applied to some students. _____
       Describe:

14. Major/Degree Areas in which general education requirements applied:

    A. Liberal Arts _____ (check appropriate
    B. Human Services _____ box)
    C. Business/Management _____

Code no. _____

D. Education _____
   E. Other: _____

   _____
   _____
   _____
   _____

15. Degrees for which general education requirements applied:

   A. All _____
   B. B.A. _____
   C. B.S. _____

16. Can you give a brief description of the previous general education requirements (if requirements differed by major or degree area, describe only those requirements that applied to the liberal arts or the B.A. program)?

17. Were there other courses required of all students? Detail:

18. How did the general education requirements change?

Code no. _____

19. NERCHE Assessment of previous general education requirements:

   0. NONE: No general education requirements   _____
   1. DIST: All req. fulfilled by student-chosen
       courses   _____
   2. MOD. DIST.: Distribution systems with
       some requirements   _____
   3. MOD. CORE: Most prescribed but some
       free course choice   _____
   4. CORE: Every course prescribed: no
       student choice   _____

20. NERCHE Assessment of degree of change from previous to current general education requirements:

   A. No change   _____
   B. Minimal change   _____
   C. Moderate change   _____
   D. Significant change _____

HISTORY OF CHANGE PROCESS

Now I would like to ask you some questions about the process the campus went through to implement the current general education requirements.

Diagnosis

21. Who was the catalyst for change? (check all who apply)
   A. President   _____
   B. Provost, Dean or VPAA   _____
   C. Faculty members   _____
   D. External actors (e.g., accr. board, state)   _____
       Specify: _____
   E. Other: _____

Code no. _____

22. What was the principal reason for the change?

23. In what year did discussion of the curriculum begin?   _____

Design

Organization of Committee(s)

24. Was a committee, task force, or other group charged with designing the change?   Y _____   N _____

25. IF YES, what kind of committee was it?

    A. Standing curriculum committee or subcommittee thereof   _____

    B. Ad hoc committee or task force   _____

    C.

Other: _____

26. Who made the appointments (title and position)?

27. What was the committee's composition?

    A. Chair of committee (title or position)

    _____

    B. No. of members on committee   _____

Code no. _____

C. Membership by title or position:

D. Reason for selecting them:

28. What was the committee's charge?

29. Over what time period did the committee meet?
FROM _____   TO _____

30. How frequently did the committee meet?

_____

31. Were there subsequent or concurrent committees?
Y ____   N ____   IF NO, GO TO Q 37.

32. IF YES, what was the committee's charge?

Code no. _____

33. What kind of committee was it? (If more than one, make appropriate distinctions.)

    A. Standing curriculum committee or subcommittee thereof   _____

    B. Ad hoc committee or task force   _____

    C. Other: _____

34. What was the composition of the committee?

    A. Chair of the committee (title or position)

    _____

    B. No. of members on committee _____

    C. Membership by title or position:

    D. Reason for selecting them:

35. Over what time period did the committee meet?
FROM _____ TO _____

36. How frequently did the committee meet?

_____

Code no. _____

Decision-Making Process

37. Did (any of) the committee(s) produce a recommendation?
Y _____   N _____

38. IF YES, describe the steps following the committee's recommendation.

39. Who had final authority to approve the proposed changes?

A.	Board of Trustees	_____
B.	President	_____
C.	Provost, Dean or VPAA	_____
D.	Faculty	_____
E.	Faculty governing body such as Faculty Senate	_____
F.	Standing curriculum committee	_____
G.	Other: _____	_____

40. Describe faculty's involvement in the debate and passage of the proposed changes.

Code no. _____

41. What, if any, was the administration's role in the debate and passage of the proposed changes?

42. Were there any factors that made the passage of the changes more difficult?

43. Were there any factors that made the passage of the changes easier?

44. What were the expected and unexpected effects of the change from the old to the new requirements?

Code no. _____

IMPLEMENTATION

45. Is there a person or committee in charge of overseeing the implementation of the general education requirements?

    A. Standing curriculum committee   _____

    B. General education committee   _____

    C. Program director   _____

    D. Dean, provost or VPAA   _____

    E. None   _____

    F. Other _____   _____

46. Were institutional resources given to any of the following as part of the implementation of the new general education requirements?

    A. Faculty incentives to create new courses   _____

    B. Faculty retraining in teaching methods or subject   _____

    C. Hiring new faculty   _____

    D. New instructional materials   _____

    E. Revisions or adjustments to advising program   _____

    F. Revisions or adjustments to new student orientation   _____

    G. Alterations in institutional mission statement   _____

    H. Alterations in admissions policies or procedures   _____

    I. Revisions to campus publications   _____

    J. Upgrading of library   _____

    K. Other _____   _____

47. If financial resources were used to implement the new general ed. requirements, where did they come from?

    A. Operating budget   _____

    B. Special institutional funds   _____

Code no. _____

C. Outside grants _____
D. Reallocation of existing institutional funds _____
E. Other: _____ _____

48. Were there any factors that made implementation of the new requirements more difficult?

49. Were there any factors that made implementation of the new requirements easier?

OVERALL ASSESSMENT

I would like to end the interview by asking you several questions about the final form of your general education requirements.

50. What effect, if any, did the following have on the design and implementation of the new general education requirements?

Mission of the college:

Code no. _____

Composition of the student body:

Financial condition of the college:

51. Were any major compromises made at any point in the process that significantly changed the design or implementation of the general education requirements?

52. Was any provision or mechanism made at any point in the process for evaluation or information gathering?

53. Is there anything not covered in the interview that might be important and help us understand the process of changing general education requirements on your campus?

Code no. _____

NERCHE ASSESSMENT OF SITE VISIT POTENTIAL

Implementation date _____

Nature of curriculum change:

Nature of process:

Special features or issues:

Concerns or drawbacks:

SITE VISIT RECOMMENDATION (record on cover page):

_____ 1 Recommended for site visit
_____ 2 Recommended with reservations
_____ 3 Not recommended for site visit

APPENDIX D

Campus Visit Questionnaire

**Implementing General Education Curriculum
New England Resource Center for Higher Education
at the University of Massachusetts Boston**

The New England Resource Center for Higher Education is conducting a study, funded by the Exxon Education Foundation, of the implementation of general education curriculum in a variety of institutions in New England. We appreciate your willingness to participate in our study. Please be assured that, unless you request otherwise, your contributions will remain anonymous in any information that is disseminated about the project.

TABLE OF CONTENTS

III. Curriculum Design Questions

Identified "historian(s)" on campus
Chair of curriculum design committee (or suitable
   substitute)
All others involved in design process

IV. Implementation Questions

Department chairs
Faculty who teach in program
Primary GE administrators
Chief academic officers/deans

I. Background Information

Name of Institution:
Name of Interviewee:
Date of Interview:
Name of Interviewer:

Let me begin by asking you some background information.

1. How long have you worked at this institution?
2. If you are a faculty member, what department are you in?
3. What jobs have you held on campus and what are the approximate dates you held each job?
4. What is your current involvement with the general education program? **Probe:** Teach in program, on committee that oversees program, on another committee?
5. In your view, what is the mission of the college?
   a. Has this mission changed over the last decade? **Probe:** Why (if yes)?
6. Characterize the student body at the college. **Probe:** Social background, academic preparation, academic interests.
   a. Has the student body changed over the last decade? Why (if yes)?

7. What are the major problems or issues facing the college?
    a. Are these the same problems or issues facing the college over the last decade?

8. How would you describe faculty morale at the college?
    a. How would you characterize the relationship between faculty and administration?

Background Information for Chief Academic Officer Only

9. How would you define the financial situation at the college?
10. Could you give me a brief history of faculty-development activities on your campus?

    Probe: Type
    When started
    Why started (target: general education?)
    Who decided
    How funded
    Frequency of activity

    a. What is the effect of faculty-development activities on the following:

        Teaching
        Student learning
        Faculty morale
        Relationships among faculty
        Relationships between faculty and
            administrators
        General education program

II. Beginning of Change Process

For Those Who Were at College at Beginning of Change Process

Now, a few questions about the beginning of the general education change process.

11. What were the primary reasons for changing the general education curriculum?

12. Were there other things happening at the time that influenced the possibility of change?

13. Who were the main catalysts of the change?

14. What were faculty's views regarding the possibility of changing the general education curriculum? **Probe:** Possible divisions along disciplinary or other organizational lines?

15. What were the administrative leadership's views toward the possibility of changing the general education curriculum? **Probe:** President, provost or VPAA, deans.

16. In your opinion, how similar or dissimilar were the faculty's and administration's views about the need for change?

III. Curriculum Design

The next set of questions focuses on designing the changes.

For Identified "Historian" on Campus Only

17. Could you give a brief outline of the sequence of events that took place between the initial proposal for change and the final policy? **Probe:** Dates.

Curriculum Design Questions for Chair of Curriculum Design Committee (or Suitable Substitute) Only

18. What kind of committee designed the general education program (standing, ad hoc or task force, other)?
    a. Who made the appointments?

19. Was the committee given a formal charge? By whom?
    a. What was the charge?
    b. Where can I get a written copy of it?

20. What was the committee's composition? **Probe:** No. of members, membership by title or position.
    a. Why were they selected?

21. Why do you think you were selected to chair the committee? (If chair not interviewed here, ask: Who chaired the committee? Why was he or she selected?)

22. What did the committee actually do?

    Probe: Overall conception
    Design of courses
    Implementation planning
    Evaluation planning
    Cost estimates

23. How frequently did the committee meet?
    a. For how long?

24. Did the committee inform the campus of its activities?
    a. If yes, describe how. **Probe:** How often, who attended, effectiveness of activities?

25. Did the committee consult with members of the campus about its recommendations?
    a. If yes, describe how. **Probe:** Who, how often, effectiveness of activities?

26. Did the committee seek advice or information from outside of the campus?
    a. If yes, describe how. **Probe:** Who, how often, effectiveness of activities?

27. What were the points of agreement and disagreement among the committee members?
    a. How did the disagreements affect the committee's deliberations?

28. Did the committee develop any recommendations?
    a. If yes, what were they?
    b. How can I get a copy?

29. What was your reaction to the committee's recommendations?

30. What happened after the committee developed its recommendations?
  a. Were the committee recommendations changed? **Probe:** When? by whom? how?

31. What was your reaction to the changes that were finally adopted?

32. Was any consideration given during this period as to how the changes would be implemented?
  a. If yes, describe. **Probe:** When? by whom? what was discussed, what was done as result?

33. What went well and not well during the period the curriculum was being designed?
  a. Finally, any important lessons that you learned in the process?

Curriculum Design Questions for All Others Involved in Design Process

34. What kind of committee designed the general education curriculum (standing, ad hoc, task force, other)?

35. What was the committee's composition?
  a. Why were they selected? **Probe:** Appropriateness of choices.

36. What did the committee designing the curriculum actually do?

37. Did the committee inform the campus of its activities?
  a. If yes, describe how. **Probe:** Who, how often, effectiveness of activities?

38. Did the committee consult with members of the campus about its recommendations?
  a. If yes, describe how. **Probe:** Who, how often, effectiveness of activities?

39. What were the points of agreement and disagreement among the committee members?

    a. How did the disagreements affect the committee's deliberations?

40. What kinds of support and opposition were expressed in the community for the committee's proposal?

41. Was faculty governance involved in reviewing the committee's recommendations?

    Probe: Who was involved?
               What did they do?
               When did they get involved?
               What was their reaction?

42. Were any revisions made by faculty governance?
    a. If yes, describe the revisions.

43. What kinds of support and opposition were expressed on the campus for the governance revisions?

44. Was any consideration given during this period as to how the changes would be implemented?
    a. If yes, describe. **Probe:** When? by whom? what was discussed, what was done as result?

45. Describe the role that the administration played during the period when the curriculum was being designed.

46. Describe the role that the faculty played during the period when the curriculum was being designed.

47. What was your reaction to the different proposals? to what was finally adopted?

48. What went well and not well during the period the curriculum was being designed?
    a. Any important lessons that you learned in the process?

IV. Implementation

The next set of questions addresses the process of implementation.

Implementation Questions for Department Chairs Only

49. Do you have any responsibility for administering the general education curriculum?
   a. If yes, describe.

50. How are faculty selected to teach in the general education program?

51. Are part-time or adjunct faculty hired to teach in the general education program?
   a. If yes, how are decisions made to hire part-time or adjunct faculty?

52. What proportion of your department's general education courses are now taught by part-time or adjunct faculty?
   a. Has this number changed over time? Explain.

53. How are general education courses proposed and selected? **Probe:** College/department decision-making process

54. Is your department or faculty compensated in any way for participating in the general education program? **Probe:** Describe compensation (stipends, release time, monies for adjunct, part-time faculty).
   a. If yes, how are general education funding decisions made?

55. Has the compensation given to your department or faculty changed over time?
   a. If yes, explain how it has changed, the reason, the effect.

56. Describe any faculty-development activity that accompanied the general education curriculum. **Probe:** Type of activity, no. of faculty in department involved, successful or not.

57. What is the effect of the general education program on the following?

Students' education
Department enrollments
Department's staffing
Course offerings
Course sizes
Faculty morale
Relations with other departments
Relations between faculty and administration

58. Have any major disagreements come up during the period that the changes have been implemented? **Probe:** Details, parties involved, resolution of disagreement.

59. Were any ideas concerning implementation rejected or contested? **Probe:** By whom, why?

60. Do you think the general education program addresses the original concerns that gave rise to the changes?

61. Does the administration support the general education program as it now exists?

62. Now that you are living with it, what are the pleasant and unpleasant surprises associated with the general education changes?

63. What went well and not well during the period the curriculum was being implemented?

    a. Any important lessons that you learned in the process?

Implementation Questions for Faculty Who Teach in Program Only

64. Describe your current teaching and advising responsibilities at the college.

    Probe: Total classes taught each semester
                 No. of general education classes
                 Average size of classes
                 No. of advisees

65. What led you to teach in the general education program?

66. What have you liked/not liked about teaching in the general education program?

    a. Do you intend to continue teaching general education courses?

67. How are faculty selected to teach in the general education program?

68. Are part-time or adjunct faculty hired to teach in the general education program?

    a. If yes, how are decisions made to hire part-time or adjunct faculty?

69. Do you think your department supports your teaching in the general education program? Explain why or why not.

70. Have you participated in any faculty-development activities associated with the general education program?

    a. If yes, have you benefited or not from these activities? If no, explain why not.

71. What additional types of faculty-development activities would you find helpful?

72. Do you think students are well advised about the program? Explain.

73. What is the effect of the general education program on the following?

Students' education
Department enrollments
Department's staffing
Course offerings
Course sizes
Faculty morale
Department relations
Relations between faculty and administration

74. How are general education courses proposed and selected? **Probe:** College/department decision-making process

75. Have any major disagreements come up during the period that the changes have been implemented? **Probe:** Details, parties involved, resolution of disagreement.

76. Were any ideas concerning implementation rejected or contested? **Probe:** By whom, why?

77. Are you satisfied with the decision-making process used to make changes in the general education program? Explain.

78. Do you think the general education program addresses the original concerns that gave rise to the changes?

79. Does the administration support the general education program as it now exists?

80. What went well and what has gone badly in implementing the general education program? **Probe:** Mistakes, good decisions.
    a. Any important lessons learned?

Implementation Questions for Primary GE Administrators Only

81. Reflecting back over the process of changing the general education curriculum, can you remember when people started to think about how to implement the changes? **Probe:** Who, when, why?

82. What person or committee is currently responsible for the general education curriculum? **Probe:** Names and positions, if appointed, reason for selection.
    a. Describe their responsibilities.

83. Has this been different in the past?
    a. If yes, describe.

84. Do department chairs have any responsibility for administering the general education curriculum?
    a. If yes, describe.

85. How is the program currently organized?

Probe: No. of sections
No. of students served
No. of full-time faculty involved by
department
No. of adjuncts and part-time faculty by
department

86. Was the program put in place all at once or phased in?
a. Describe the reason for this decision.

87. Do departments participate equally in the general education program?
a. If not, explain why.

88. Describe how decisions are made about the amount of resources given to the general education program.
a. Has the amount of resources given to the general education program changed? **Probe:** How, why?

89. Do you think the resources have been sufficient? Explain why or why not.

90. Have any major disagreements come up during the period that the changes have been implemented? **Probe:** Details, parties involved, resolution of disagreement.

91. Were any ideas concerning implementation rejected or contested? **Probe:** By whom, why?

92. Have there been any important changes in the program since it became policy? **Probe:** What, why?

93. Is there an effort to evaluate the program? If no, are there plans to do so?
a. If yes, describe the evaluation method.

Probe: *Purpose:* changes in individual student learning, effectiveness of dept./college/ GE program
Design: course evaluations, student tests/ portfolios, survey of faculty/students, etc.
Form: standard test or home-grown instrument, outside evaluation, etc.

94. Do you think the general education program addresses the original concerns that gave rise to the changes?

95. Does the administration support the general education program as it now exists?

96. Now that you are living with it, what are the pleasant and unpleasant surprises associated with the changes?

97. What went well and what has gone badly in implementing the general education program? **Probe:** Mistakes, good decisions?

     a. Any important lessons learned?

Implementation Questions for Chief Academic Officer/Deans Only

98. Reflecting back over the process of changing the general education curriculum, can you remember when people started to think about how to implement the changes? **Probe:** Who, when, why?

99. What person or committee is currently responsible for the general education curriculum? **Probe:** Names and positions, if appointed, reason for selection.

     a. Describe their responsibilities.

100. Has this been different in the past?

     a. If yes, describe.

101. Was the program put in place all at once or phased in?

     a. Describe the reason for this decision.

102. Do departments participate equally in the general education program?

     a. If not, explain why.

103. Describe how decisions are made about the amount of resources given to the general education program.

     a. How are decisions made about the *allocation* of these resources?

104. Has the amount of resources given to the general education program changed?

    a. If yes, explain how the resources have changed, the reason for the change.

105. Do you think the resources have been sufficient? Explain why or why not.

106. Have any major disagreements come up during the period that the changes have been implemented? **Probe:** Details, parties involved, resolution of disagreement.

107. Were any ideas concerning implementation rejected or contested? **Probe:** By whom, why?

108. Have there been any important changes in the program since it became policy? **Probe:** What were the changes, why?

109. Is there an effort to evaluate the program? If not, are there plans to do so?

    a. If yes, describe the evaluation method.

> **Probe:** *Purpose:* changes in individual student learning, effectiveness of dept./college/ GE program
> *Design:* course evaluations, student tests/ portfolios, survey of faculty/students, etc.
> *Form:* standard test or home-grown instrument, outside evaluation, etc.

110. Do you think the general education program addresses the original concerns that gave rise to the changes?

111. Does the administration support the general education program as it now exists?

112. Now that you are living with it, what are the pleasant and unpleasant surprises associated with the changes?

113. What went well and what has gone badly in implementing the general education program? **Probe:** Mistakes, good decisions?

    a. Any important lessons learned?

Bibliography

Abrams, Douglas. (1993). *Conflict, competition or cooperation: Dilemmas of state education policymaking.* Albany, NY: State University of New York Press.

Adelman, Clifford. (1994). *Lessons of a generation: Education and work in the lives of the high school class of 1972.* San Francisco: Jossey-Bass.

Aldrich, Howard E. (1979). *Organizations and environments.* Englewood Cliffs, NJ: Prentice-Hall.

Allison, Graham T. (1971). *Essence of decision: Explaining the Cuban missile crisis.* Boston: Little, Brown.

American Council on Education. (1988). *Campus trends.* Washington, DC: Author.

American Council on Education. (1989). *1989–90 fact book on higher education.* New York: Macmillan.

American Council on Education. (1992). *Campus trends, 1992.* Washington, DC: Author.

American Council on Education. (1994). *Campus trends, 1994.* Washington, DC: Author.

Arnold, Gordon B. (1994). *General education curriculum decision making in organizational context: The revision of the Boston College core curriculum, 1989 to 1991.* Unpublished doctoral dissertation, Boston College, Chestnut Hill, MA.

Association of American Colleges. (1985). *Integrity in the college curriculum: A report to the academic community.* Washington, DC: Author.

Association of American Colleges. (1994). *Strong foundations: Twelve principles for effective general education programs.* Washington, DC: Author.

Astin, Alexander W., & Lee, Calvin B. T. (1972). *The invisible colleges: A profile of small, private colleges with limited resources.* New York: McGraw-Hill.

Baldridge, J. Victor. (1971). *Power and conflict in the university: Research in the sociology of complex organizations.* New York: Wiley.

Baldridge, J. Victor, & Deal, Terrence (Eds.). (1982). *The dynamics of organizational change in education.* Berkeley, CA: McCutchan.

Barrow, Clyde. (1993). Will the fiscal crisis force higher education to restructure? *Thought and Action: The NEA Higher Education Journal, 9* (1), 7–24.

Becker, William. (1990). The demand for higher education. In Stephen Hoenack & Eileen L. Collins (Eds.), *The economics of American universities: Management, operations and fiscal environment* (pp. 155–188). Albany, NY: State University of New York Press.

Bellah, Robert N., Madsen, Richard, Sullivan, William M., Swidler, Ann, & Tipton, Steven M. (1985). *Habits of the heart: Individualism and commitment in American life.* Berkeley, CA: University of California Press.

Bennett, William J. (1984). *To reclaim a legacy: A report on the humanities in higher education.* Washington, DC: National Endowment for the Humanities.

Bensimon, E. M., & Neumann, A. (1993). *Redesigning collegiate leadership: Teams and teamwork in higher education.* Baltimore: Johns Hopkins University Press.

Bensimon, E. M., Neumann, A., & Birnbaum, R. (1989). *Making sense of administrative leadership: The "L" word in higher education.* Washington, DC: George Washington University, School of Education and Human Development. (ERIC Clearinghouse on Higher Education.)

Birnbaum, Robert. (1985). State colleges: An unsettled quality. In Study Group on the Conditions of Excellence in American Higher Education, *Contexts for learning: The major sectors of American higher education* (pp. 17–31). Washington, DC: U.S. Department of Education.

Birnbaum, Robert. (1988). *How colleges work: The cybernetics of academic organization and leadership.* San Francisco: Jossey-Bass.

Bolman, L. G., & Deal, T. E. (1984). *Modern approaches to understanding and managing organizations.* San Francisco: Jossey-Bass.

Boyer, Ernest L., & Levine, Arthur. (1991). *A quest for common learning: The aims of general education.* Washington, DC: Carnegie Foundation for the Advancement of Teaching.

Breneman, David W. (1990). Are we losing our liberal arts colleges? *College Board Review, 156,* 16–21, 29.

Breneman, David W. (1994). *Liberal arts colleges: Thriving, surviving, or endangered?* Washington, DC: The Brookings Institution.

Breneman, David W. (1995, Sept. 8). Sweeping, painful changes. *The Chronicle of Higher Education,* 111–112.

Brinkman, Paul. (1990). College and university adjustments to a changing financial environment. In Stephen Hoenack & Eileen L. Collins (Eds.), *The economics of American universities: Management, operations and fiscal environment* (pp. 215–232). Albany, NY: State University of New York Press.

Burke, Kenneth. (1969). *A rhetoric of motives.* Berkeley, CA: University of California Press.

Burns, J. M. (1978). *Leadership.* New York: Harper & Row.

Carnegic Council on Policy Studies in Higher Education. (1980). *Three thousand futures: The next twenty years for higher education.* San Francisco: Jossey-Bass.

Carnegie Foundation for the Advancement of Teaching. (1977). *Missions of the college curriculum: A contemporary review with suggestions.* San Francisco: Jossey-Bass.

Carnegie Foundation for the Advancement of Teaching. (1982). *The control of the campus.* Lawrenceville, NJ: Princeton University Press.

Carnegie Foundation for the Advancement of Teaching. (1987). *A classification of institutions of higher education.* Princeton, NJ: Author.

Carnegie Foundation for the Advancement of Teaching. (1990). *Campus life: In search of community.* Princeton, NJ: Author.

Carnegie Foundation for the Advancement of Teaching. (1994). *A classification of institutions of higher education.* Princeton, NJ: Author.

Carnochan, W. B. (1993). *The battleground of the curriculum: Liberal education and the American experience.* Stanford, CA: Stanford University Press.

Chaffee, Ellen Earle. (1984). Successful strategic management in small private colleges. *Journal of Higher Education, 55,* 212–241.

Clark, Burton. (1983). *The higher education system: Academic organization in cross-national perspective.* Berkeley, CA: University of California Press.

Clotfelter, Charles, Ehrenberg, R., Getz, M., & Siegfried, J. (1991). *Economic challenges in higher education.* Chicago: University of Chicago Press.

Cohen, M. D., & March, J. G. (1974). *Leadership and ambiguity: The American college president.* New York: McGraw-Hill.

Cohen, Michael D., March, James G., & Olsen, Johan P. (1972). A garbage can model of organizational choice. *Administrative Science Quarterly, 17,* 1–25.

Delbanco, Andrew. (1995, Mar. 27). Contract with academia. Comment, *New Yorker Magazine, 71,* 7.

DiMaggio, Paul J., & Powell, Walter W. (1983). The iron cage revisited: Institutional isomorphism and collective rationality in organizational fields. *American Sociological Review, 48,* 147–160.

Donahue, James A. (1990). Jesuit education and the cultivation of virtue. In William J. O'Brien (Ed.), *Jesuit education and the cultivation of virtue* (pp. 51–71). Washington, DC: Georgetown University Press.

Dunham, E. Alden. (1969). *Colleges of the forgotten Americans: A profile of state colleges and regional universities.* New York: McGraw-Hill.

Edelman, Murray. (1964). *The symbolic uses of politics.* Urbana, IL: University of Illinois Press.

Fairweather, James. (1989). Academic research and instruction: The industrial connection. *Journal of Higher Education, 60,* 388–407.

Feldman, Martha S. (1989). *Order without design: Information production and policy making.* Stanford, CA: Stanford University Press.

Finkelstein, Martin J., Farrar, D., & Pfnister, Allan. (1984). The adaptation of liberal arts colleges in the 1970s: An analysis of critical events. *Journal of Higher Education, 55,* 242–268.

Finnegan, Dorothy E. (1991). *Opportunity knocked: The origins of contemporary comprehensive colleges and universities.* Working Paper #6. New England Resource Center for Higher Education, University of Massachusetts Boston.

Finnegan, Dorothy E., & Gamson, Zelda F. (1996). The adoption of the research culture in comprehensive institutions: An analysis of disciplinary adaptations. *Review of Higher Education, 19,* 141–147.

Freeland, Richard M. (1992). *Academia's golden age: Universities in Massachusetts 1945–1970.* New York: Oxford University Press.

Froomkin, Joseph. (1990). The impact of changing levels of financial resources on the structure of colleges and universities. In Stephen Hoenack & Eileen L. Collins (Eds.), *The economics of American universities: Management, operations and fiscal environment* (pp. 189–214). Albany, NY: State University of New York Press.

Gaff, Jerry G. (1983). *General education today: A critical analysis of controversies, practices, and reforms.* San Francisco: Jossey-Bass.

Gaff, Jerry G. (1991). *New life for the college curriculum.* San Francisco: Jossey-Bass.

Gamson, Zelda F. (1987). An academic counter-revolution: The roots of the current movement to reform undergraduate education. *Educational Policy,* 429–444.

Gamson, Zelda F. (1992). The realpolitik of reforming general education. *Proceedings of the Asheville Institute on General Education* (pp. 70–72). Washington, DC: Association of American Colleges.

Gamson, Zelda F., & Associates. (1984). *Liberating education.* San Francisco: Jossey-Bass.

Gamson, Zelda F., Kanter, Sandra, & London, Howard. (1992). General education reform: Moving beyond the rational model of change. *Perspectives, 22,* 58–68.

Gilbert, Joan. (1995, Sept./Oct.). The liberal arts college—Is it really an endangered species? *Change,* 37–43.

Grant, Gerald (Ed.). (1979). *On competence: A critical analysis of competence-based reforms in higher education.* San Francisco: Jossey-Bass.

Grant, Gerald, & Riesman, David. (1978). *The perpetual dream: Reform and experiment in the American college.* Chicago: University of Chicago Press.

Grant, W. Vance, & Eiden, Leo J. (1982). *Digest of education statistics 1982.* Washington, DC: Government Printing Office.

Gross, Edward, & Etzioni, Amitai. (1985). *Organizations in society.* Englewood Cliffs, NJ: Prentice-Hall.

Halperin, Morton H. (1974). *Bureaucratic politics and foreign policy.* Washington, DC: The Brookings Institution.

Halstead, Kent. (1995). *Rich colleges, poor colleges.* Washington, DC: Research Associates of Washington.

Hammond, Martine R. (1984). Survival of small private colleges: Three case studies. *Journal of Higher Education, 55,* 360–388.

The Harvard Committee. (1945). *General education in a free society: Report of the Harvard Committee.* Cambridge, MA: Harvard University Press.

Hefferlin, J. B. Lom. (1969). *Dynamics of academic reform.* San Francisco: Jossey-Bass.

Higher Education Publications. (1991). *1991 Higher education directory.* Washington, DC: Author.

Hines, Edward. (1988). *Higher education and state government: Renewed partnership, cooperation or competition?* College Station, TX: Association for the Study of Higher Education. (ASHE-ERIC Education Reports.)

Hirschman, Albert O. (1970). *Exit, voice, and loyalty: Responses to decline in firms, organizations, and states.* Cambridge, MA: Harvard University Press.

Hoenack, Stephen, & Collins, Eileen L. (Eds.). (1990). *The economics of American universities: Management, operations and fiscal environment.* Albany, NY: State University of New York Press.

Jencks, Christopher, & Riesman, David. (1968). *The academic revolution.* New York: Doubleday.

Kanter, Rosabeth, Stein, Barry, & Jick, Todd. (1992). *The challenge of organizational change: How companies experience it and leaders guide it.* New York: The Free Press.

Kanter, Sandra, London, Howard, & Gamson, Zelda. (1991). The implementation of general education: Some early findings. *Journal of General Education, 40,* 119–132.

Keller, G. (1983). *Academic strategy: The management revolution in American higher education.* Baltimore: Johns Hopkins University Press.

Keller, Phyllis. (1982). *Getting at the core: Curricular reform at Harvard.* Cambridge, MA: Harvard University Press.

Keppel, Francis. (1987). The Higher Education Acts contrasted, 1965–1986: Has federal policy come of age? *Harvard Educational Review, 57* (1), 49–67.

Kerr, Clark. (1966). *The uses of the university.* New York: Harper & Row.

Kerr, Clark. (1991). *The great transformation in higher educa-tion: 1960–1980.* Albany, NY: State University of New York Press.

Kerr, Clark. (1994). *Troubled times for American higher edu-cation: The 1990's and beyond.* Albany, NY: State Univer-sity of New York Press.

Kimball, Bruce A. (1986). *Orators and philosophers: A history of the idea of liberal education.* New York: Teachers Col-lege Press.

Kingdon, John W. (1984). *Agendas, alternatives, and public policies.* Boston: Little, Brown.

Lasswell, Harold D. (1936). *Politics: Who gets what, when, how.* New York: McGraw-Hill.

Leslie, Larry, et al. (1990). *ASHE reader on finance in higher education.* Needham Heights, MA: Ginn Press.

Levine, Arthur. (1978). *Handbook on undergraduate curricu-lum: Prepared for the Carnegie Council on Policy Studies in Higher Education.* San Francisco: Jossey-Bass.

Levine, Arthur (Ed.). (1993). *Higher learning in America, 1980–2000.* Baltimore: Johns Hopkins University Press.

Lewis, Laurie, & Farris, Elizabeth. (1989). Undergraduate general education and humanities requirements. In *Higher Education Surveys*, Report No. 7. Rockville, MD: Westat.

March, James G. (1982). Emerging developments in the study of organizations. *Review of Higher Education, 6* (1), 1–17.

March, J. G., & Olsen, J. P. (1979). *Ambiguity and choice in organizations.* Bergen, Norway: Universitetsforlaget.

March, J. G., & Olsen, J. P. (1989). *Rediscovering institutions: The organizational basis of politics.* New York: The Free Press.

McLaughlin, Judith Block, & Riesman, David. (1990). *Choos-ing a college president: Opportunities and constraints.* Princeton, NJ: Carnegie Foundation for the Advancement of Teaching.

Meyer, John W., & Rowan, Brian. (1977). Institutionalized

organizations: Formal structure as myth and ceremony. *American Journal of Sociology, 83,* 340–363.

Miller, Gary. (1988). *The meaning of general education: The emergence of a curriculum paradigm.* New York: Teachers College Press.

Miller, Perry. (1956). *Errand into the wilderness.* Cambridge, MA: Belnap Press of the Harvard University Press.

Munson, Fred C., & Pelz, Donald C. (1982). *Innovating in organizations: A conceptual framework.* Ann Arbor, MI: University of Michigan.

National Commission on Excellence in Education. (1983). *A nation at risk: The imperative for educational reform.* Washington, DC: Government Printing Office.

National Endowment for the Humanities in Higher Education. (1984). *To reclaim a legacy: A report on the humanities in higher education.* Washington, DC: Government Printing Office.

National Policy Board of Higher Education Institutional Accreditation. (1994). *Independence, accreditation, and the public interest.* Washington, DC: Author.

Nordvall, Robert C. (1982). *The process of change in higher education institutions.* Washington, DC: American Association for Higher Education. (AAHE-ERIC/Higher Education Research Report No. 7.)

Perkin, Harold. (1984, July/Aug.). Defining the true function of the university: A question of freedom versus control. *Change* (16), 20–21, 28–29.

Peters, Thomas J., & Waterman, Robert H., Jr. (1982). *In search of excellence: Lessons from America's best-run companies.* New York: Harper & Row.

Peterson, Marvin, (Ed.). (1991). *Organization and governance in higher education: An ASHE reader* (4th ed.). Needham, MA: Ginn Press.

Peterson, Marvin, Blackburn, Robert T., & Gamson, Zelda F. (1978). *Black students on white campuses: The impacts of increased black enrollments.* Ann Arbor, MI: University of

Michigan, Institute for Social Research, Survey Research Center.

The Pew Higher Education Roundtable. (1994). To dance with change. *Policy Perspectives, 5* (3), Section A. Philadelphia: Author.

Pfeffer, Jeffrey. (1981). *Power in organizations.* Marshfield, MA: Pitman.

Pfeffer, Jeffrey, & Salancik, Gerald R. (1978). *The external control of organizations: A resource dependence perspective.* New York: Harper & Row.

Pfnister, Allan O. (1984). The role of the liberal arts college: A historical overview of the debates. *Journal of Higher Education, 55,* 145–170.

Pfnister, Allan O. (1985). The American liberal arts college in the eighties: Dinosaur or phoenix? In Study Group on the Conditions of Excellence in American Higher Education, *Contexts for learning: The major sectors of American higher education* (pp. 33–48). Washington, DC: U.S. Department of Education.

Powell, Walter W. (1988). Institutional effects on organizational structure and performance. In Lynne G. Zucker (Ed.), *Institutional patterns and organization* (pp. 115–136). Cambridge, MA: Ballinger.

Reports on the course of instruction in Yale College: By a committee of the corporation and the academical faculty. (1828). New Haven, CT: Howe.

Riesman, David, Gusfield, Joseph, & Gamson, Zelda. (1970). *Academic values and mass education: The story of Oakland and Monteith.* New York: Doubleday.

Rockefeller Foundation. (1979). *Toward the restoration of the liberal arts curriculum.* New York: Author.

Rowse, Glenwood, & Wing, Paul. (1982). Assessing competitive structures in higher education. *Journal of Higher Education, 6,* 656–686.

Rudolph, Frederick. (1962). *The American college and university: A history.* New York: Knopf.

Rudolph, Frederick. (1977 and 1993). *Curriculum: A history of the American undergraduate course of study since 1636.* San Francisco: Jossey-Bass.

Sergiovanni, T. J., & Corbally, J. E. (Eds.). (1987). *Leadership and organizational culture: New perspectives on administrative theory and practice.* Urbana, IL: University of Illinois Press.

Seymour, D. T. (1988). *Developing academic programs: The climate for innovation.* College Station, TX: Association for the Study of Higher Education. (ASHE-ERIC Higher Education Report No. 3.)

Seymour, Daniel. (1989). Maximizing opportunities through external relationships. *New Directions for Higher Education, 68,* 5–23. San Francisco: Jossey-Bass.

Simon, Kenneth A., & Grant, W. Vance. (1973). *Digest of education statistics 1972.* Washington, DC: National Center for Education Statistics, Government Printing Office.

Smelser, Neil J. (1987). Collective myths and fantasies. In Jerome Rabow, Gerald M. Platt, & Marion S. Goldman (Eds.), *Advances in psychoanalytic sociology* (pp. 316–328). Malabar, FL: Kreiger.

Snyder, Thomas D., & Hoffman, Charlene M. (1994). *Digest of education statistics 1994.* Washington, DC: National Center for Education Statistics, Government Printing Office.

Steiner, David M. (1994). *Rethinking democratic education: The politics of reform.* Baltimore: Johns Hopkins University Press.

Study Group on the Conditions of Excellence in American Higher Education. (1984). *Involvement in learning: Realizing the potential of American higher education.* Washington, DC: U.S. Department of Education.

Thatcher, Sanford G. (1991). Publisher's note. *Journal of General Education, 40,* ix–xvii.

Tierney, W. G. (1989). *Curricular landscapes, democratic vistas: Transformative leadership in higher education.* New York: Praeger.

Tierney, William (Ed.). (1991). *Culture and ideology in higher education: Advancing a critical agenda*. New York: Praeger.

Traub, James. (1994). *City on a hill: Testing the American dream at City College*. Reading, MA: Addison-Wesley.

Turner, Sarah E., & Bowen, William G. (1990). The flight from the arts and sciences: Trends in degrees conferred. *Science, 250,* 517–521.

U.S. Department of Health, Education and Welfare. (1963). *Digest of education statistics 1963*. Washington, DC: Government Printing Office.

Weaver, Frederick Stirton. (1991). *Liberal education: Critical essays on professions, pedagogy, and structures*. New York: Teachers College Press.

Weick, Karl E. (1976). Educational organizations as loosely coupled systems. *Administrative Science Quarterly, 21,* 1–19.

White, Charles. (1994). A model for comprehensive reform in general education: Portland State University. *Journal of General Education, 43,* 168–229.

Wilshire, Bruce. (1990). *The moral collapse of the university: Professionalism, purity, and alienation*. Albany, NY: State University of New York Press.

Wuest, Francis J. (1979). *Renewing liberal education: A primer*. Kansas City, MO: Change in Liberal Education Network.

Zucker, Lynne G. (1983). Organizations as institutions. In S. B. Bacharach (Ed.), *Research in the sociology of organizations* (vol. 2) (pp. 1–47). Greenwich, CT: JAI Press.

Zucker, Lynne G. (1987). Institutional theories of organization. *Annual Review of Sociology, 13,* 443–464.

Zucker, Lynne G. (Ed.). (1988). *Institutional patterns and organizations: Culture and environment*. Cambridge, MA: Ballinger.

Zumeta, William. (1995). State policy and budget developments. In *The NEA 1995 almanac of higher education* (pp. 73–96). Washington, DC: NEA.

Index

(Cont.)

Faculty perception of reform,
35
Implementation after state
college board of trustees
action, 43
Influence of environment on, *23*
New five-year program, 43
Proposal for general education
reform, 41–42

Kean College of New Jersey, 35,
38–40, 60
Demographics of college, 39
Description of college, 38–39
Implementation of program, 40
Influence of environment on, *23*
Proposal for general education
program, 39
Recommendations for further
change, 40
Kerr, Clark, 17

Lasswell, Harold D., 76
Leadership, impact of wise, 128
Legitimacy, politics of. See Politics
of legitimacy
Liberal arts
Departments, as losers in
competition for scarce
resources, 8
Departments, strength of, in
general education movement,
10
Faculty representing, dominance
on design committee, 46
Fate of, 1
Professional degrees awarded at
liberal arts colleges, 1972,
1988, 7
And quality of student learning,
119
Reinvigoration of, at University
of Minnesota, Morris, 111
And studies and projects by
national associations, 1, 9
Lines of demarcation, as aspect of

general education issues, 82
Loyalty, or willingness to compromise, 95

"Management by committee," 63
Mass higher education, 2
Mellon, Andrew W., Foundation,
36, 92
Meyer, John W., 97 *n*
Miller, Perry, 118 *n*
*Missions of the College Curricu-
lum*, 5, 8
Muscatine, Charles, 108

National associations, studies and
projects in general education,
1, 9
National Endowment for the
Humanities, 33–34, 56, 90,
92
National general education move-
ment, 8–10
National model, of prestigious
colleges and universities, 4
New England Association of
Schools and Colleges, 27, 55,
56, 65
New England College, 24–25,
27–28, 35
Description of college, 27
Implementation of changes,
27–28
Influence of environment on, *24*
Modification of new curriculum,
28
Proposal for general education
reform, 27
New faculty positions, 112
Nonelite institutions, as stepping-
stone to more prestigious
institutions, 6

Occupational training and skills, 5
Open design of general education
programs, as characteristic of
successful reform, 127, 129